To Pauline
with love
at Christmas 2005.
golden

ELGIN

A HISTORY AND CELEBRATION
OF THE TOWN

MARY BYATT

Produced by The Francis Frith Collection
exclusively for

OTTAKAR'S

www.ottakars.co.uk

First published in the United Kingdom in 2005
by The Francis Frith Collection®

Hardback Edition 2005
ISBN 1-84567-744-7

British Library Cataloguing in Publication Data

Elgin - A History and Celebration of the Town
Mary Byatt

The Francis Frith Collection
Frith's Barn, Teffont,
Salisbury, Wiltshire SP3 5QP
Tel: +44 (0) 1722 716 376
Email: info@francisfrith.co.uk
www.francisfrith.co.uk

Printed and bound in England

Front Cover: **ELGIN, LITTLE CROSS 1890** E56004t

Additional modern photographs by Mary Byatt.

Domesday extract used in timeline by kind permission of
Alecto Historical Editions, www.domesdaybook.org
Aerial photographs reproduced under licence from
Simmons Aerofilms Limited.
Historical Ordnance Survey maps reproduced under licence from
Homecheck.co.uk

Every attempt has been made to contact copyright holders of
illustrative material. We will be happy to give full acknowledgement
in future editions for any items not credited. Any information should
be directed to The Francis Frith Collection.

*The colour-tinting in this book is for illustrative purposes only,
and is not intended to be historically accurate*

Contents

ELGIN FROM THE AIR 1955 AFR23872

Historical Timeline for Elgin

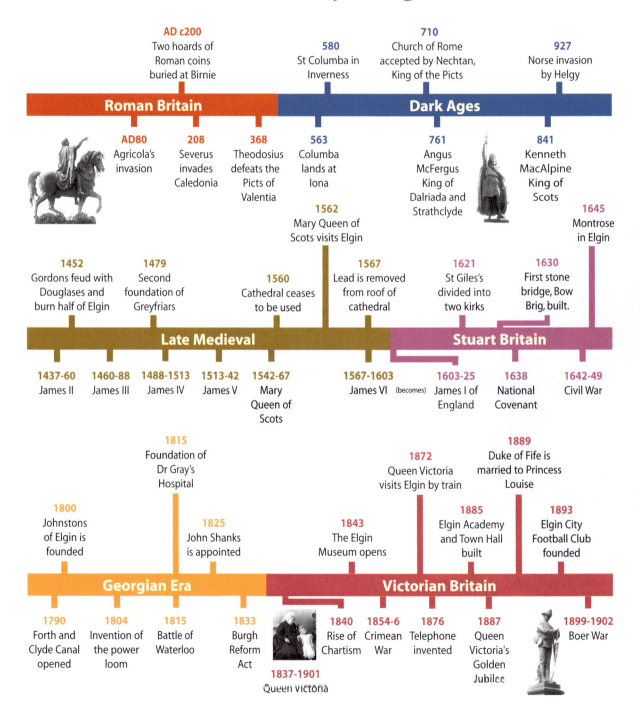

AD c200
Two hoards of
Roman coins
buried at Birnie

580
St Columba in
Inverness

710
Church of Rome
accepted by Nechtan,
King of the Picts

927
Norse invasion
by Helgy

Roman Britain

Dark Ages

AD80
Agricola's
invasion

208
Severus
invades
Caledonia

368
Theodosius
defeats the
Picts of
Valentia

563
Columba
lands at
Iona

761
Angus
McFergus
King of
Dalriada and
Strathclyde

841
Kenneth
MacAlpine
King of
Scots

1562
Mary Queen of
Scots visits Elgin

1645
Montrose
in Elgin

1452
Gordons feud with
Douglases and
burn half of Elgin

1479
Second
foundation of
Greyfriars

1560
Cathedral ceases
to be used

1567
Lead is removed
from roof of
cathedral

1621
St Giles's
divided into
two kirks

1630
First stone
bridge, Bow
Brig, built.

Late Medieval

Stuart Britain

1437-60
James II

1460-88
James III

1488-1513
James IV

1513-42
James V

1542-67
Mary
Queen of
Scots

1567-1603
James VI   (becomes)

1603-25
James I of
England

1638
National
Covenant

1642-49
Civil War

1815
Foundation of
Dr Gray's
Hospital

1872
Queen Victoria
visits Elgin by train

1889
Duke of Fife is
married to Princess
Louise

1800
Johnstons
of Elgin is
founded

1825
John Shanks
is appointed

1843
The Elgin
Museum opens

1885
Elgin Academy
and Town Hall
built

1893
Elgin City
Football Club
founded

Georgian Era

Victorian Britain

1790
Forth and
Clyde Canal
opened

1804
Invention of
the power
loom

1815
Battle of
Waterloo

1833
Burgh
Reform
Act

1840
Rise of
Chartism

1854-6
Crimean
War

1876
Telephone
invented

1887
Queen
Victoria's
Golden
Jubilee

1899-1902
Boer War

1837-1901
Queen Victoria

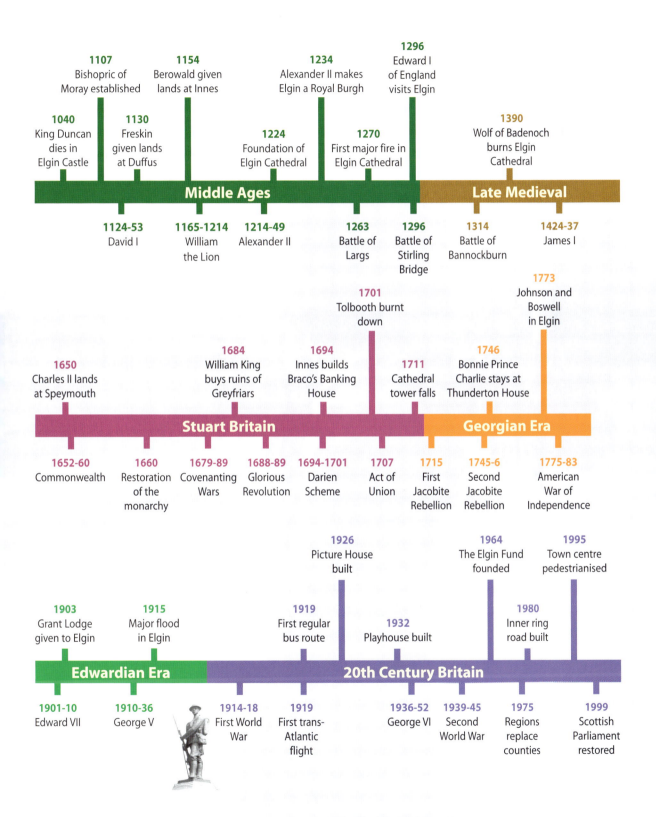

Middle Ages

1107 Bishopric of Moray established

1154 Berowald given lands at Innes

1234 Alexander II makes Elgin a Royal Burgh

1296 Edward I of England visits Elgin

1040 King Duncan dies in Elgin Castle

1130 Freskin given lands at Duffus

1224 Foundation of Elgin Cathedral

1270 First major fire in Elgin Cathedral

Late Medieval

1390 Wolf of Badenoch burns Elgin Cathedral

1124-53 David I

1165-1214 William the Lion

1214-49 Alexander II

1263 Battle of Largs

1296 Battle of Stirling Bridge

1314 Battle of Bannockburn

1424-37 James I

Stuart Britain

1701 Tolbooth burnt down

1773 Johnson and Boswell in Elgin

1650 Charles II lands at Speymouth

1684 William King buys ruins of Greyfriars

1694 Innes builds Braco's Banking House

1711 Cathedral tower falls

1746 Bonnie Prince Charlie stays at Thunderton House

Georgian Era

1652-60 Commonwealth

1660 Restoration of the monarchy

1679-89 Covenanting Wars

1688-89 Glorious Revolution

1694-1701 Darien Scheme

1707 Act of Union

1715 First Jacobite Rebellion

1745-6 Second Jacobite Rebellion

1775-83 American War of Independence

Edwardian Era

20th Century Britain

1926 Picture House built

1964 The Elgin Fund founded

1995 Town centre pedestrianised

1903 Grant Lodge given to Elgin

1915 Major flood in Elgin

1919 First regular bus route

1932 Playhouse built

1980 Inner ring road built

1901-10 Edward VII

1910-36 George V

1914-18 First World War

1919 First trans-Atlantic flight

1936-52 George VI

1939-45 Second World War

1975 Regions replace counties

1999 Scottish Parliament restored

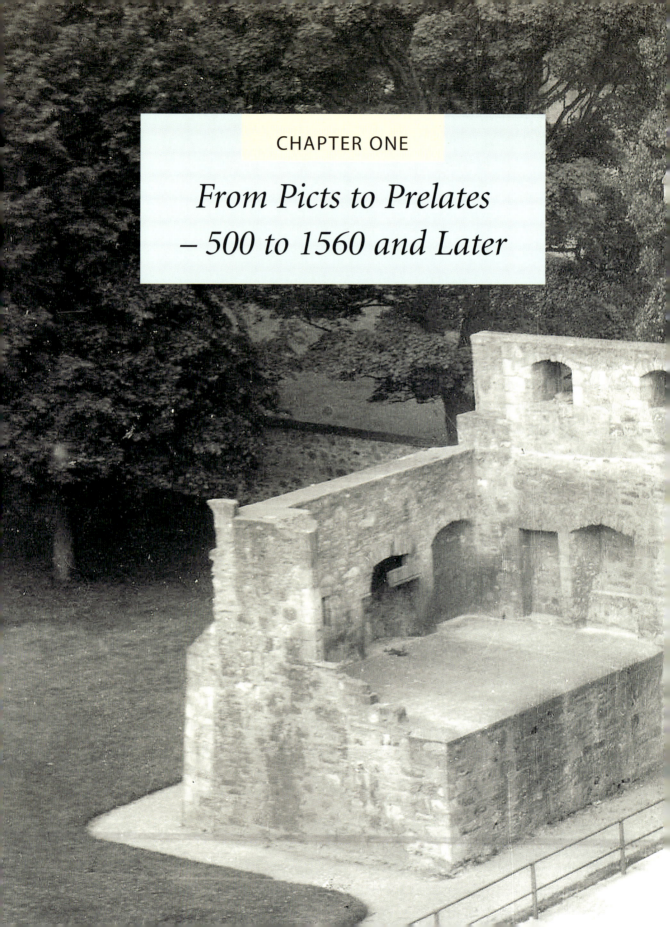

CHAPTER ONE

From Picts to Prelates – 500 to 1560 and Later

IN THE RUINS of Elgin Cathedral at the east end of Elgin stands a remarkable granite cross-slab from the Dark Ages. This stone is known as the Elgin Pillar, and was discovered in 1823, when the foundations were being dug for the new church of St Giles in the centre of Elgin. Whilst its true significance is not known, the historian H B Mackintosh ventured to suggest that it might be the original Elgin market cross. It represents the very beginnings of Christianity in Elgin and shows the incorporation of Christian beliefs with the ancient symbolism of the Picts. Both sides of the stone have Pictish carvings on them; one side is decorated with pagan symbols, and the other with a cross. The Christian side of the stone has four figures holding books, one in each quadrant of the cross. Two of the figures are identifiable by their accompanying symbols, Saint Matthew with his angel and Saint John with his eagle. Perhaps the other two are Saint Mark and Saint Luke, but the carving is really too worn to identify them.

ELGIN CATHEDRAL, THE CHOIR
c1890 E56001

The Elgin Pillar is on the left.

THE ELGIN PILLAR ZZZ04293
(From: 'Early Christian Monuments of Scotland')

Note the hunting scene of the time, with four horsemen and three hounds pursuing a stag. The principal horseman has a hawk on his outstretched arm, and one of the hounds is in the act of seizing the stag by the flank.

Pictish Stones

The Picts left no written history, but their enigmatic symbol stones occur all over the northeast of Scotland. The stones are classed according to the type of engraving on them. Class I stones are rough-hewn stones with incised carving on one side only. The famous Burghead bulls are examples of these. This particular bull is in the Elgin Museum; it is used in the logo of the Moray Society, which owns and runs the museum. Class II stones are shaped stone slabs carved in relief on both sides. Many have Pictish symbols on one side and a Christian cross on the other, as in the Elgin Pillar.

A BURGHEAD BULL 2005 ZZZ04294 (Mary Byatt)

Some say that Christianity was brought to Moray by St Columba and his monks in around AD 580, but there is no evidence that St Columba ever visited the area in person. The first known Culdee (Scotto-Irish) church in the area was Birnie Church, two miles south of Elgin, and although it is dedicated to St Brendan the Navigator, it is not thought that he came to Moray.

From about AD 710, the Church of Rome and its religious hierarchy were accepted in Pictland, but the Bishopric of Moray was not established until 1107. Moray's first bishop, Gregorius, took charge of the Culdee churches of Birnie, Kinnedar, and Spynie. Birnie was the seat (cathedra) of the first four bishops. Kinnedar then briefly became the cathedral, followed by Spynie in 1207, where a college of eight canons was established. The constitution of the prelates was modelled on that of Lincoln Cathedral and copied into the Register of

Moray. Later on Lincoln is said to have lost its own statutes, and copied them back from Moray. Bishop Bricius (1203-1222) felt that Spynie was too isolated, and asked Pope Honorarius if the cathedral could be moved to the Church of the Holy Trinity 'juxta' Elgin. His request was granted, but by then there was a new bishop, Andrew de Moravia. The first stone of the cathedral was laid on 19 June 1224 and consecrated by the Bishop of Caithness. Bishop Andrew had visited Lincoln Cathedral, and through him its influence was felt in the design of Elgin Cathedral.

> The principal members of the Chapter were:
>
> 1. The Dean, who presided over 10 canons and was the chairman of the chapter.
> 2. The Arch-Deacon or Sub-Dean who visited the diocese and examined candidates for holy orders.
> 3. The Chanter or Precentor, who presided over the choir and was in charge of all music.
> 4. The Chancellor, who was the bishop's lawyer, secretary to the chapter and keeper of their seal.
> 5. The Treasurer, who was in charge of the revenues of the bishop.
>
> Each of these dignitaries had designated outlying parishes that supported them.

'Lamp of the North'

'Queen of our Northern minsters, raised to be
  A Scottish Lincoln, by the high-born priest
Who, copying Hugo's statutes, saw the feast
  Spread out by Gothic builders - verily
Art made to wait on worship, wherefore he
  Returning home a gorgeous
structure planned.'
  (The Very Rev James Cooper DD, c1915)

Bishop Andrew increased the size of the college to 23 canons, and it remained at this number for the next 300 years. He died in 1242, and was buried under a slab of blue marble on the south side of the choir.

ELGIN CATHEDRAL

The increase in power and resources of the bishops of Moray was rapid. In 1115, the first bishop would have had a clay-built or wooden church and residence. Little more than a century later, Elgin had one of the most magnificent churches of the kingdom as the cathedral church of the diocese. It stood at the extreme border of civilisation on the edge of the Highlands, where the countryside was relatively uncultivated. Most people lived in temporary wooden huts, making the splendour of Elgin Cathedral even more amazing.

'Nobilis et decora ecclesia Moraviensis speculum patriae et decus regni' ('Noble and beautiful church of Morayshire, mirror of our land and the glory of our kingdom').
  (Probably by Bishop Bur c1390)

The building of the cathedral was under the patronage of King Alexander II of Scotland, a frequent visitor to Elgin between 1221 and 1244. At that time, incorporations of 'free' masons, furnished with Papal bulls, travelled across Europe taking with them the art of building cathedrals. It is thought that they brought their skills to Elgin too. In 1235 Alexander II founded a chapel in the cathedral for the soul of Duncan, who was wounded by Macbeth at Bothgowan (Pigaveny) in 1040 and is said to have died in Elgin Castle. Alexander II also founded the hospital of Maison Dieu, the friaries of the Black Friars and the Grey Friars, and the Benedictine priory of Pluscarden.

The cathedral had a chequered history, and was damaged and re-built many times. The oldest part of the cathedral is the south wall of the south transept, and may well be part of the original Church of the Holy Trinity. Its Gothic architecture is of the Transitional period between Norman and the first pointed style, typical of the beginning of the 13th century in Scotland. The lower stages of the west towers are also very old. The chapter house is of the late pointed style, whilst the nave was reconstructed in the Decorated period.

A fire in 1270 caused the first major damage to the cathedral, and resulted in extensive rebuilding. The chapter house, choir aisles and southwest porch were added during the restoration that followed. Over a century later, the cathedral was damaged again. The notorious Alexander Stewart, 'the Wolf of Badenoch', brother of Robert III, quarrelled with the then Bishop of Moray, Alexander Bur, who disapproved of his extra-marital affair. The Wolf then seized the Bishop's lands in Badenoch and was excommunicated as a result.

ELGIN CATHEDRAL, THE WEST TOWERS FROM THE CHOIR c1890 E56003

In 1390, the vengeful Wolf descended from his castle in Lochindorb with his 'Wyld Wykkyd Heland-men' and burned the town of Forres and its church. From there they moved on to Elgin, where they burnt the whole town, eighteen manses, the Maison Dieu and the cathedral. Many books, charters and valuable possessions of the county were lost in the fire. The central tower was destroyed, resulting in the loss of the cathedral's fine profile. It took seventy years of continuous work to make good the damage. The chapter house needed a complete interior casing of masonry and new windows. It owes its survival after the Reformation to the fact that the trades used it as a meeting place.

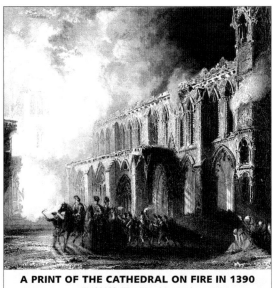

A PRINT OF THE CATHEDRAL ON FIRE IN 1390
EM00002 (The Elgin Museum)

THE ROOF OF THE CHAPTER HOUSE 1878 SA000202 (Courtesy of University of St Andrews Library)

The ribbed vaulting springing from a central column was added c1490.

THE CHAPTER HOUSE 2005 E56701k (Mary Byatt)

Bishop Bur appealed to King Robert III for help, referring to the cathedral as 'the special ornament of the country, the glory of the Kingdom, the delight of strangers and the praise of visitors', and saying that 'its fame was known and lauded even in foreign lands on account of the multitude of its servitors and its most fair ornaments'. As a result, the king appears to have made an annuity of £20 'during the King's pleasure'. In subsequent years, bishops themselves contributed to the restoration and were required to pay one third of their revenue towards the cost of reconstruction.

The central tower was rebuilt in 1407 by Bishop John Innes, but it collapsed in 1506 and was rebuilt again by Bishop Patrick Hepburn in 1538. The cathedral now had a splendid steeple 198 feet high. The rose window in the arch above the great west door was added in 1423 by Bishop Columba, in line with the fashion of the day. Some of the tracery of this window has been found, together with a tracing on stone of its original design. A drawing has been made of its reconstruction, and striking similarities have been found to a rose window in the east front of the Nine Altars chapel in Fountains Abbey in Yorkshire.

AN IMAGINARY ENGRAVING OF ELGIN CATHEDRAL BEFORE 1560 BY SLEZER IN 1693 EM00003 (The Elgin Museum)

This was drawn partly from the ruins as they were in the late 17th century and partly from records.

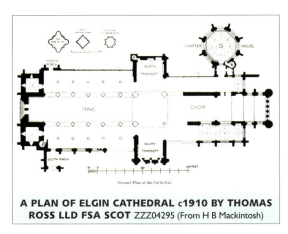

A PLAN OF ELGIN CATHEDRAL c1910 BY THOMAS ROSS LLD FSA SCOT ZZZ04295 (From H B Mackintosh)

THE CATHEDRAL, THE GREAT WEST DOOR
EM00004 (The Elgin Museum)

At its height, Elgin Cathedral was said to be the finest church in Scotland, combining size and ornament without rival. Its total length was 289 feet, making it the third largest cathedral in Scotland after St Andrews and Glasgow. Its large five-aisled nave - an arrangement found otherwise only in Chichester - must have given a feeling of great spaciousness, and the great west doorway, split by a central column, recalls those of French cathedrals.

The Wolf of Badenoch's actions were by no means the last foul treatment of Elgin in the Middle Ages. In July 1402, during the period of re-construction of the cathedral, Alexander Macdonald 'spulzied' (plundered) the Chanonry and made off with some of the remaining wealth of the cathedral. It was obviously worth his while, because he returned to repeat the exercise in October 1402. This time he was met by the bishop and the entire chapter and persuaded to repent. He was punished on the site of the Little Cross, and gave money for 'a cross and a bell'.

THE COLLEGE OF THE CHANONRY

Surrounding the cathedral was a walled precinct known as the College of the Chanonry, containing the manses of its associated clergy. The college precinct was once surrounded by a massive stone wall, 6½ feet wide, 12 feet high and 2700 feet long. It had four entrance gates or ports: the West Port, opening into the town, the North Port, crossing the Bishop's Road at the back of the Bishop's Palace, the South Port, lying opposite the Bede Houses in South College Street, and the East or Panns Port, opening to the meadowland known in 1566 as 'Le Pannis'. Study of the remains of Panns Port (now Pansport) shows that unwanted intruders were kept out by a portcullis and heavy wooden doors. The whole structure must have been twice the height it is now to accommodate the lifting mechanism for the portcullis.

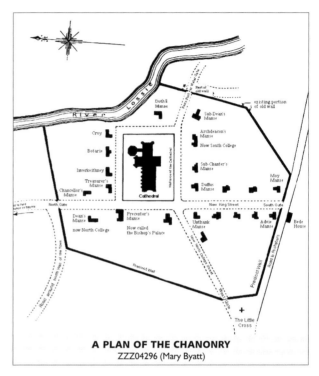

A PLAN OF THE CHANONRY
ZZZ04296 (Mary Byatt)

This plan shows the College of the Chanonry as it was when the cathedral was at its height.

PANNS PORT 1839 ZZZ04299 (D Alexander)

THE BISHOP'S PALACE c1910 EM00005 (The Elgin Museum)

This building is more correctly termed the Precentor's Manse.

Within this wall were the manses and gardens of the canons. Each building was in the style of a tower-house and maintained by 'appropriation' of parochial teinds (tithes) collected throughout the diocese of Moray. The manse with the quaintest name, Unthank Manse, was the manse of the canonry of Unthank, whose supporting parish included Duffus Castle and its chapel dedicated to the Blessed Virgin Mary. Other manses in the Chanonry included Botarie, Inverkeithing, Croy, the Treasurer's, the Chancellor's and the Dean's. Of these, only the Dean's house remains, and is now known as the North College - or just the College. It was transformed in 1858 into a comfortable house.

A fine example of 15th-century architecture can be seen in the remains of the Bishop's Palace (or more correctly the Precentor's Manse) on the edge of the Cooper Park. It probably replaced an older residence where the bishop would have stayed whilst overseeing the rebuilding of the cathedral. Spynie Palace to the north of Elgin was always the main residence of the Bishops of Moray. Some use of the Precentor's manse by bishops is documented - Bishop William Spynie is known to have died there in 1406, and Bishop Patrick Hepburn added the south wing in 1557.

Following the reformation, the Bishop's Palace was given to Alexander Seton, along with Pluscarden Abbey. Seton was made Lord High Chancellor for Scotland in 1604 and 1st Earl of Dunfermline in 1606. He named the Bishop's Palace Dunfermline House, and greatly enlarged it. He was Provost of Elgin from 1591 to 1607 and Provost of Edinburgh from 1598 to 1608. He died in 1622.

The 4th Earl of Dunfermline also added to the house, but he was then outlawed for fighting at Killecrankie. His estate passed to the Crown and was purchased by the Duke of Gordon in 1730. Later, the house (by then roofless) passed to the Seafield family, who would have pulled it down but for the intervention of members of the Elgin Society in the 20th century. It was then gifted to the city by the Dowager Countess of Seafield and re-roofed. There is a trinity of heads on the skew-put (the cornerstone supporting the gable coping) on the east wall of the staircase - apparently there is a similar one in Amiens, France.

THE TRINITY OF FACES 2005 E56702k (Mary Byatt)

The carving can be seen on a skew-put on the Bishop's Palace.

OTHER RELIGIOUS ESTABLISHMENTS

THE FRIARIES

Unlike monks, whose monasteries were in secluded places, friars lived in towns, caring for the poor, the outcast and the lepers. The Grey Friars and the Black Friars were two mendicant orders (living off alms) introduced to Elgin by Alexander II. Both considered the reading and writing practised by monks as superfluous luxuries.

The Black Friars were the preaching friars, or Dominicans, who professed poverty and self-denial with great zeal. They wore dark habits. The history of their order in Elgin is scant, but they may have been established around 1233. By the 16th century they had acquired wealth, and their property at Black Friars' Haugh consisted of a manor place, houses, yards and orchards. All of this would have been set alight at the time of the Reformation in 1560, but the buildings were not finally razed to the ground until 1750. When the ruins were removed, many coins, seals, rings and antique silver spoons were found and sold in Edinburgh. (See Langs Seals Vol II 1142). The name Blackfriars lives on as the name of an area down by the river in the west of the town.

The Grey Friars were Franciscans and wore grey habits. They witnessed against the covetousness and luxury that came of wealth. No charter exists of the original foundation of the Grey Friars in Elgin, but by the mid 13th century they were known to have a spacious church and fine buildings. It would seem that they were not well provided for in terms of food; evidence for this is a charter granting them '2 davats of land in Ross at Kattepel' (now Cadboll). If the friars chose not to stay in Elgin, the revenue from this land was to be put to support two chaplains in the cathedral. Presumably they left Elgin, for by the time of Bishop John Winchester (1437-58) two chaplains existed with funding from Kattepel.

The present much-restored Greyfriars buildings belong to a later foundation, that of John Innes in 1479. Unlike the original foundation, it was well-supported and lasted for 81 years up until the time of the Reformation in 1560, when the Earl of Huntly, Master of Moray, invaded Elgin and laid waste its religious houses. The Grey Friars' monastery was actually set on fire by Alexander Innes, grandson of its founder. The old Greyfriars' kirk must have retained its roof, as it was used as a courthouse at the end of the 16th century – there was no Tolbooth at that time. A century later, the buildings passed out of the Innes family's hands, and the Old Kirk was used as a meeting place for the Trades from 1676 to 1691. After that the Trades returned to meeting in the chapter house again. In 1684 the property was bought by William King, later Provost of Elgin. It remained with the King family and their descendants for the next two hundred years, and many monuments to members of the King family adorn the walls of the Greyfriars Kirk.

THE RUINS OF GREYFRIARS KIRK c1880 EM00006 (The Elgin Museum)

Did you know?

The mummified cat in the Elgin Museum was found in the walls of Greyfriars church when it was restored at the end of the 19th century. Walling up a live cat was a protective omen in medieval times.

In 1891, the property was bought by the Sisters of Mercy and so passed back into Catholic hands. The 3rd Earl of Bute (a Catholic) funded its restoration, and the architect John Kinross provided the elegant timber vaulted roof, the splendid rood screen and the carved oak stalls in the choir. The property is still owned by the Sisters of Mercy, and features pleasant stone cloisters surrounding the original well. It is said that traces of medieval painting can still be seen in the rafters of the refectory. The restored Greyfriars is the best example of a medieval priory in Scotland.

THE RESTORED GREYFRIARS KIRK IN THE EARLY 20TH CENTURY EM00007 (The Elgin Museum)

THE LEPER HOUSE

Leprosy was likely to have been introduced by the Crusaders in the 10th and 11th centuries. Like most towns, Elgin had a leper house for isolation of lepers. It is known to have been at Pinefield on the east of Elgin. In the mid 19th century a large amount of stone was dug up at Hospital Croft, near the Fochabers road, which might well have been the remains of the leper house. At least forty cartloads of stones were removed, some being large boulders that appeared to have been set in blue clay.

THE MAISON DIEU

The old medieval hospital of Maison Dieu was established around 1237 in the reign of Alexander II as an almshouse with chapel for 'poor brothers and sisters' of the neighbourhood. After the Reformation it fell into ruins, but in 1620 James VI granted a charter for the re-building of the Maison Dieu. Thereafter it supported a teacher of 'music and other liberal sciences', and looked after a few poor. It was one of two schools chiefly maintained by the revenues of the town. By 1750 it seems to have become ruined again and was destroyed by a hurricane.

THE BEDE HOUSES

The Bede Houses were almshouses under the fraternity of the Maison Dieu, and were supported by its revenues until the Reformation. In 1624, when the Maison Dieu lands had been given to the town, the magistrates built a Bede House on the south side of South College Street. Four bedemen (destitute burghers) lodged there with their

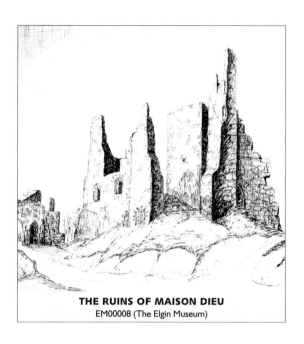

THE RUINS OF MAISON DIEU
EM00008 (The Elgin Museum)

THE INSCRIPTION ON THE STONE TABLET ON THE BEDE HOUSES 1816   ZZZ01300 (I I D Mackintosh)

wives and were paid £18 a year. They wore a string of beads, and were obliged to utter as many prayers daily for their benefactors as there were beads on the string. It was recorded in 1638 that the bedemen had to attend morning and evening prayers every day 'or otherwise salbe put out of their place.' In 1788 the Town Council supplied them with special blue gowns. The Bede House of 1624 fell into ruins and was rebuilt in 1846. It was replaced again in the 1970s, and the inscribed tablet from above the door of the 1846 Bede House was retained and set into the wall.

THE BISHOPS OF MORAY

The Bishopric of Moray was a great prize of the church, and given only to statesmanlike men of quality and virtue. It lasted 581 years, with a succession of admirable bishops. One such was Bishop David, who in 1313 decided to send four poor scholars to the University of Paris. By 1325, the idea was well endowed, and there were so many Scots in Paris that the Scots College was set up.

Bishop Robert Reid

Robert Reid was born in 1528 at Aikenhead, perhaps near Lossiemouth, (though there are many Aikenheads in Scotland). He had a distinguished career both in state diplomacy and in the church, where he was onetime sub-dean of Elgin Cathedral, Abbot of Kinloss (1528) and Bishop of Orkney (1540) – indeed, the inscription around the edge of his bookplate reads 'Robertus Reid Episcopus Orchadensis et Abbas Akynlos 1558'. In 1533, he was sent by the King of the Scots to seek peace with Henry VIII. In 1558 he went to France to witness the marriage of Mary Queen of Scots to the Dauphin. The cost of this embassy was £2,000 Scots, of which Elgin had to pay £25 6s 3d. Abbot Reid returned to Kinloss with Guillaume Lubias, a one-legged gardener from Dieppe, who was skilled in the grafting of fruit trees. Lubias revolutionised the growing of fruit both at Kinloss and throughout the Laich of Moray. Robert Reid died 1559, leaving £450 to the town of Edinburgh for establishing a 'schola illustris'. The money was used to establish the College of Edinburgh from which Edinburgh University grew.

BISHOP ROBERT REID'S BOOKPLATE 1558
ZZZ04301 (Records of the Monastery of Kinloss 1872)

The last Roman Catholic Bishop of Moray was Bishop Patrick Hepburn, and he most certainly did not have the attributes of his predecessors. He lived a dissolute life; he is said to have boasted of having a dozen mistresses, seven of them being other men's wives. He saw the approach of the Reformation, and transferred much of the church lands in his care to his numerous relatives. He retired to Spynie Palace, fortified it and stayed there, living in splendour until his death in 1573.

BISHOP PATRICK HEPBURN'S ARMS 2005
ZZZ04302 (Mary Byatt)

The coat of arms is carved on a stone slab in the southernmost of the cathedral's two west towers. Colours have been added as they would have been in medieval times.

THE REFORMATION

The Reformation dissolved the medieval church order. The cathedral ceased to be used, and the manses were secularised. The revenues of the chaplainries, the friaries and the Maison Dieu all passed to the Town Council for community use. In February 1567 the Regent of Moray and his Privy Council ordered the lead to be removed from the roof of the cathedral. It was sold to a mercantile firm in Amsterdam to provide money to pay the regent's army and was lost at sea off Aberdeen, together with the lead from Aberdeen's own cathedral. Dr Johnson wrote in 1773: 'Every reader will rejoice that this cargo of sacrilege was lost at sea'. From then on the cathedral was left to decay. On 4 December 1637 'ane horrible high wind' blew down the rafters. In 1640, the General Assembly ordered the removal of the wooden rood screen 'painted in excellent colouris illuminat with starris of bricht golde'. It was brought down by the Minister of St Giles and by the young lairds of Innes and Brodie. The minister took the timber home to burn in his kitchen, but it refused to stay alight - an omen noted by his servant. In 1640, some painted rooms still remained in the towers and beside the choir; they were so complete that they were still used by Roman Catholics for worship. The cathedral's central tower fell in 1711, and for the next 100 years the townsfolk took stone from it to build their houses and used the site as a dump. In the words of Dr Samuel Johnson, who stayed in Elgin in 1773, the Cathedral 'was at last not destroyed by the tumultuous violence of Knox, but more shamefully suffered to dilapidate by deliberate robbery and frigid indifference.'

The privilege of being buried in the cathedral once belonged to the bishop and chapter, but from the middle of the 17th century it became the general cemetery for the parish. There are many fine and interesting tombs in the graveyard, some having been transferred there from the churchyard of Old St Giles, in the centre of Elgin, when the new church was built. Meanwhile the cathedral continued to decay.

'Wind scarred and crumbling
 'neath the tread of time,
Thy walls still rear their venerable bulk,
 As gaunt and battered ribs
from out the slime,
 Reveal the noble bark - a stranded hulk.'
(Alex Geddie c1905)

In the 19th century, the shame of this wreck was realised. A 'drouthy cobbler' named John Shanks was appointed Keeper of the Cathedral in 1825, under the direction of Isaac Forsyth, bookseller and eminent citizen of Elgin. The whole site was buried in rubble and rubbish; Shanks managed to remove 2866 barrow loads of litter by hand to a deep pool known as the Order Pot before the Morayshire Farmers' Club sent him a horse and cart. Shanks discovered and excavated the original steps leading to the great west door, and after that the Crown Authorities subscribed handsomely to the excavation of the whole cathedral to its original

ground-floor level. The Board of Works paid for a new roof for the chapter house and iron bands to secure the west towers. The cathedral and its cemetery were enclosed in iron railings and a lodge built for the keeper.

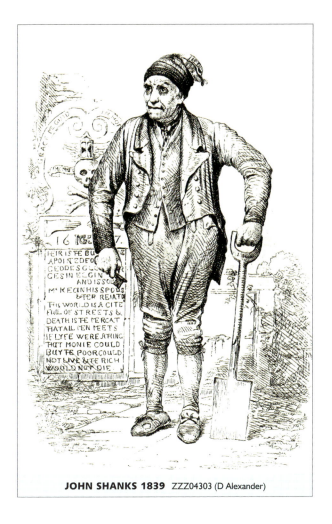

JOHN SHANKS 1839　ZZZ04303 (D Alexander)

John Shanks is standing in front of a well-known gravestone of a glover in the cathedral's graveyard. Inscribed on it is:
'This world is a cite full of streets &
Death is the mercat that all men meets.
If life were a thing that monie could buy,
The poor could not live and the rich could not die'.

The spirit and energy of John Shanks returned the cathedral site to some of its former glory. In February 1899, Henry F Kerr ARIBA wrote in The Builders Journal and Architectural Record: 'There is grace of design, superb proportion, the utmost delicacy of detail and although there is ample ornament, there is none without repose and restraint which makes the work most fascinating'. To this day, the cathedral ruins retain a majesty all of their own and continue to be a source of wonder for visitors from all over the world.

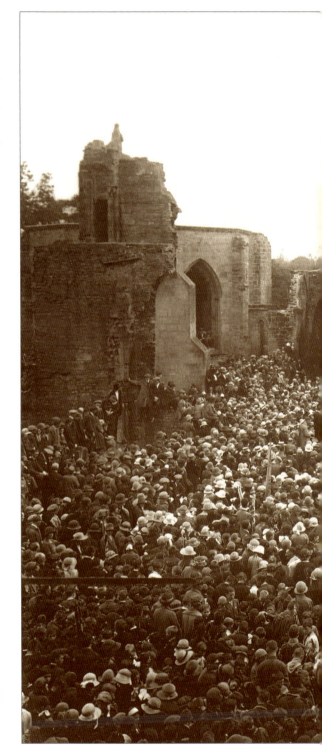

ELGIN CATHEDRAL 1924   EM00009 (The Elgin Museum)

This photograph shows the service marking the 700th anniversary of the foundation of Elgin Cathedral in 1924.

Coffie

Gaufy

Brouinsyde Ogftoun Ettills Ernhill
K: of Ogftoun Steefold
Pleulands Newtoun
K: of Kirtedwart
K: of Duffus Meovetou Akinhead Inch
Drany Speyflaw
Duffous Caft Ardiuet Cotts Vmhan Brandftou
Balormy
Moftowy Spyny Newtoun Bun hill
Liggeit The Stainwells
Quarelwood Loch of Carfe
Moffack R. Park of Quarelwood Finrefs Innefs Caft Brie
Innerlochtys Myirfy d Caft: of Spyny wate
Morniftoun Caldhem Pitgeuny Barnyards
Pindreeh Shi-Feftul Barnethills Coldcotts Leuthars N: Mefs Aem
ELGINN S: Andrews K: O: Mefs
Kirkhill Balloly Vrchart
Baefrukty Fofterfeate Scotfouhill K: of Vrwhart
Maine N: Linkwod Shererftou Mi
Loffy R. Byres K: of Lambry Thraipland
K: of Birnay Glaffrefh Bugs Wood Coftou Caft Petinfeir
Linkwod Byres
Trowis Whynnas
boig Halzou
Miltoun Cotts L: na Bo.
Kirktoun of Langmorne Thornhil
B: of Linkwod Clachmarras
Whytwrae Blackhills

Gedlocch

Broun Moore B: of Douald ou Blackburne

CHAPTER TWO

Kings, Barons and Burghers – 1000 to 1799

ONE OF ELGIN'S unchanging and enduring landmarks is the green mound called Ladyhill at the west end of the town. On the top of Ladyhill are the ruins of Elgin Castle. Like most medieval castle sites, that of Elgin makes use of a natural feature with a commanding view. Ladyhill rises steeply from the flood plain of the river Lossie on its southern side, and overlooks a level plateau on which the burgh was established.

The first castle here would have been just an earth and wood structure. The current ruins are of a stone building constructed by King David I when he took control of Moray in 1130.

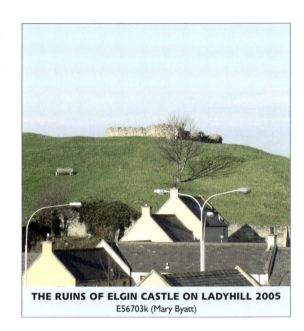

THE RUINS OF ELGIN CASTLE ON LADYHILL 2005
E56703k (Mary Byatt)

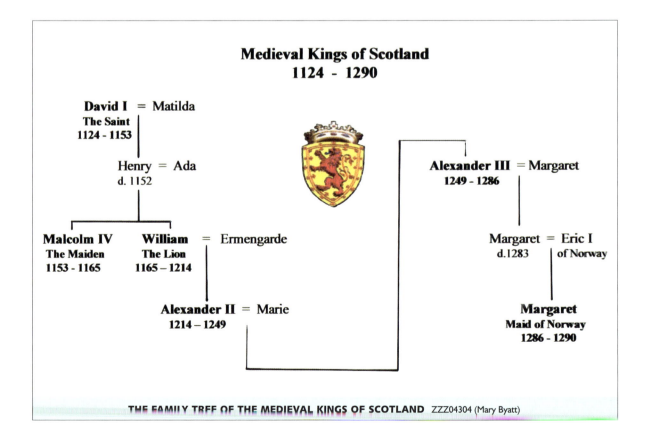

THE FAMILY TREE OF THE MEDIEVAL KINGS OF SCOTLAND   ZZZ04304 (Mary Byatt)

Controlling Moray was difficult for the Scots king, isolated as it was by rivers and mountains. Emulating William the Conqueror in England, the king gave large tracts of land to foreign barons, whose duty it then was to keep the natives under control. Two of these barons were Freskin and Berowald from Flanders. Freskin was sent north by David I in 1130 to quell an uprising in Moray. He was given land to the north of Elgin, where he built Duffus Castle. David I spent the summer of 1150 at Duffus Castle, supervising the building of Kinloss Abbey. In 1154 Malcolm IV succeeded his grandfather to the throne, and one year later granted Berowald lands at Innes and Easter Urquhart, both to the east of Elgin. To prevent the barons from becoming too powerful, the Scots kings were canny and gave land to the church too, to act as a buffer.

The castle of Elgin became the centre of royal authority for Moravia (Moray), which at one time stretched right across to the west coast of Scotland. William the Lion occasionally held court in the castle, and is said to have granted no less than 14 charters to the Burgh of Elgin, compared to only one granted to Inverness and six to Aberdeen. One of his charters names the Burgh as 'Helgyn', a name associated by some people with Helgy, a Norse general who invaded Scotland in AD 884. Helgy could have named the settlement after himself, but since Elgin existed long before 884, the theory has been discredited. William the Lion did not stay in Elgin as often as his son, Alexander II, who did more to promote the interests of Elgin than any other monarch. It was he who created the Royal Burgh of Elgin.

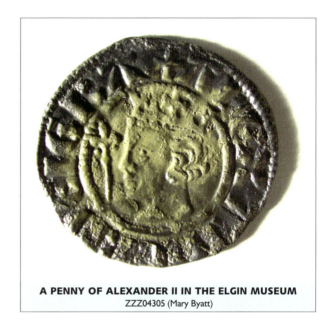

A PENNY OF ALEXANDER II IN THE ELGIN MUSEUM
ZZZ04305 (Mary Byatt)

Alexander II came to Elgin many times between 1221 and 1242 to enjoy hunting in the royal forests around Elgin. Elgin Cathedral was built during his reign, and he is said to have also founded Elgin's other religious establishments, the Maison Dieu, Blackfriars, Greyfriars and Pluscarden Abbey. Alexander's visits were not usually in the winter, but he is known to have spent Christmas at Elgin Castle in 1231. A large garden supplied the King's kitchen, and was looked after by a gardener called William (Willielmus Ortulanus).

Alexander III succeeded to his father's throne in 1249 and is said to have spent some time in Elgin Castle in 1261. During his stay, Robert Spine, Keeper of the

Cross Bows (balistarius), proved his right of tenure to the king's garden. He claimed that it had belonged to his wife's ancestors on condition that they supplied the castle kitchen with 'potherbs' during the king's stay and also took charge of his gerfalcons and goshawks while he was in residence. For this they were paid 'a chalder' of meal yearly and a daily allowance of 2d for feeding each gerfalcon and 1d for each goshawk - a delightful insight into the life of the times.

When Alexander III died in 1286, the nearest heir to the throne was his three-year-old Norwegian granddaughter. His son had predeceased him, and his daughter, who had married Eric II of Norway, had also died. This left Eric's tiny daughter, Margaret, as heir to the Scottish throne. Known as the Maid of Norway, this poor child died from seasickness on the way over from Norway in 1290. There followed controversy over who was to be her rightful heir, and the ambitious King Edward I of England took advantage of the situation.

He endorsed John Balliol, a great-grandson of David I, as Margaret's successor, but established himself as feudal overlord in Scotland. Balliol was crowned King John at Scone, but Edward took every opportunity to humiliate him. In 1295, Balliol made a treaty with France, initiating 'the auld alliance', and Edward was incensed. He moved north in 1296, sacked the town of Berwick with a cruelty that was extreme even by medieval standards, and caught up with Balliol at Brechin. There he literally stripped the royal arms off the King's tunic and claimed the crown for himself. Balliol was then imprisoned in the Tower of London, where he earned the nickname 'toom tabard' (empty coat). King Edward proceeded on to Elgin with 5,000 armed horsemen and 30,000 foot-soldiers. He stayed in Elgin Castle, by now a substantial building 3 or 4 storeys high, and his army camped outside the town. He remained in Elgin for only three days, but during this time many distinguished individuals from all over Scotland travelled to Elgin to make submission to him. He succeeded in getting the Burghers and Community of Elgin to take an oath of fealty, and to renounce all confederacies with France.

When Edward left, he put Reginald de Chen of Duffus in charge of a garrison at Elgin Castle. On his way back to Westminster, he visited the Abbey of Scone, where he ransacked the archives and carried away the Scottish regalia and the Stone of Destiny upon which kings of Scotland had been

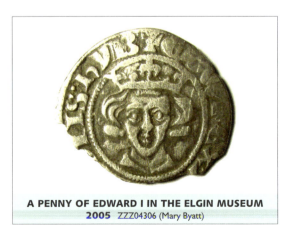

A PENNY OF EDWARD I IN THE ELGIN MUSEUM
2005 ZZZ04306 (Mary Byatt)

crowned for some 800 years. The Stone of Destiny was put under the coronation chair in Westminster Abbey, and was not returned to Scotland until 1996. It is now in Edinburgh Castle.

Edward's activities infuriated the Scots, and by the summer of 1297 a full-scale revolt had broken out. William Wallace led the patriots in the south, whilst Andrew Murray regained the castles of Forres, Elgin and Duffus in the north. In September Wallace and Murray joined forces and defeated the English army at the Battle of Stirling Bridge. Wallace's war cry was 'Scotland and Freedom', and after his victory he took the title of Guardian of Scotland. Andrew Murray was wounded and later died. Edward continued to hammer the Scots during the following year, and finally defeated Wallace at Falkirk in 1298. Wallace then went underground for seven years.

Edward moved north again in 1303 and entered Elgin once more at the head of a great force. He is said to have stayed at Duffus Manse in the Chanonry this time, the castle having been burnt by Andrew Murray when he retook it from Edward's men in 1297. Duffus Manse was one of the manses of the canons, and was built on ground that had once belonged to the cathedral's glaziers (the Vitrearius family).

Edward's control of Scotland was short-lived. Robert the Bruce, great-great grandson of David I, claimed the Scottish throne and had himself crowned King Robert I in 1306. Edward I died a year later and was succeeded by his ineffectual son, Edward II. By 1314,

Stirling was the only castle in Scotland still in English hands. Robert the Bruce made use of strategic ground behind the Bannockburn at Stirling and defeated Edward's 20,000 strong army with a much smaller force.

Elgin's troubles were not always with the English. Some 150 years after the battle of Bannockburn, a local feud between the Gordons and the Douglases resulted in half of Elgin being burnt down. The west half of Elgin supported the Douglases, so in 1452 the Gordons destroyed it. Legend has it that this half of the town stretched to the west of the castle. It was never rebuilt, and the town then expanded to the east, filling the space between it and the Chanonry. During the Douglas rebellion of 1457, Archibald Douglas, Earl of Moray, lost his life and the earldom became forfeited to the crown. The young King James II spent some time in Moray after that, and gave the earldom of Moray to his infant son, David. He directed certain districts to be left untilled so he could hunt them, and he is said to have carefully reimbursed the tenants of that land. He stayed in Elgin at Duffus Manse with his kinsman David Stewart. While he was there the kitchen was destroyed by fire, and he gave money for a new one. David Stewart later became Bishop of Moray and built 'Davy's tower', a well-known feature of Spynie Palace.

James IV, grandson of James II, was another king who greatly enjoyed hunting in the forests around Elgin. He came to Elgin several times between 1494 and 1504 to shoot stags, goats and wild boar. Later on in the 16th century, Mary Queen of Scots stayed in both Elgin and Spynie. After the death of Elizabeth I in 1603, Mary's son, James VI of Scotland, became heir to the throne of England, making him James I of England. So the crowns became united under one monarch, although the two parliaments remained separate for another hundred years.

James VI of Scotland and I of England died in 1625 and was succeeded to the throne by his son, Charles. In 1638, Charles I caused disturbances in Scotland by decreeing that the new Book of Common Prayer be used throughout the land. The nobles of

Scotland took great exception to this. They produced what was known as the 'National Covenant', rejecting the new liturgy. They sent commissioners all around Scotland to get people to sign the Covenant, and they arrived at Elgin on 13 April 1638. A few years later, another covenant was formulated in which the Scots pledged their allegiance to the Parliamentary Party of England on condition that the Anglican Church be reformed. This was the 'Solemn League and Covenant', and Charles I accepted it. Montrose went north to suppress the popular uprising in the northeast. He passed through Moray in 1645, charging all men between 16 and 60 to rise up and serve

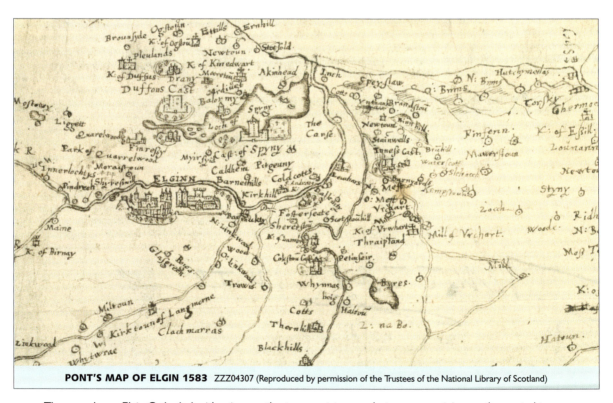

PONT'S MAP OF ELGIN 1583 ZZZ04307 (Reproduced by permission of the Trustees of the National Library of Scotland)

The map shows Elgin Cathedral with spires on the two west towers, but none remaining on the central tower.

King Charles. He plundered and burned the property of any that refused. Everyone in Elgin was terrified as Montrose and his army approached. The Fastern E'en (pre-Lenten) market of 1645 was in full swing when word came that Montrose was approaching, and it was discharged by 'tuck of the drum' lest the people 'get skaith' (injured). Everyone hurried home. A deputation of lairds visited Montrose, now camped in Elgin, and gave him 4,000 merks to spare the town from being burned. In spite of this, Montrose's soldiers (especially the Grants) plundered the town pitifully.

Charles II landed at Speymouth on 23 June 1650 and was persuaded to sign the Solemn League and Covenant there. He most probably bypassed Elgin and went on south in his quest to restore the monarchy. The Scots assisted him, but the campaign was defeated by the English army.

Cromwell's troops were frequently in Elgin between 1650 and 1660. During this time they were quartered in the cathedral, where they mutilated the carvings and figures of saints and angels and left bullet holes in the walls.

BURGHS AND ROYAL BURGHS

It was David I who first established burghs in Scotland, granting them charters to trade and so improve the economy of the area. Among those burghs was Elgin.

The early Burgh of Elgin had a population of some five or six hundred burghers. They had considerable power to regulate their everyday affairs, but were under the overall

Scottish Burghs

Burgh is a Scottish word for a chartered town. The citizens of a burgh were known as burghers; prominent citizens were honoured by being made a burgess of the town, and were then presented with a burgess seal. Elgin first had burgesses in the 15th century, and there was usually a roll of about thirty of them at any one time. The 1706 Convention of the Burghs gave the Town Council a constitution. The Town Council was to consist of 17 members, including a Deacon Convener and two Deacons of the Trades, chosen by the council. The office-bearers were the Provost, four Bailies and a Treasurer. Three members of the Guildry and two of the Trades were to stand down at the annual elections. The status of Scottish burghs was abolished in 1975.

control of the King's Sheriff in the castle. They lived in timber structures, set at right angles to the one street. Each house had a 'toft' of land behind it, ten paces wide. The tofts extended north and south to the boundary wall of the burgh. They were used for stabling and crafting, and they also provided space to keep a cow or a pig and room to grow food.

Some one hundred years after David I established the Burgh of Elgin, Alexander II elevated it to a Royal Burgh. Elgin then became the most important town north of Aberdeen - even more important than Inverness. The Town Council was now presided over by a Lord Provost. The burghers had a merchant guild, giving them a monopoly of trade throughout the Sheriffdom of Elgin. There were trade links with other free burghs of northern Scotland, forming a 'hanse'. The Royal Burgh of Elgin now had the privilege of raising revenue by means of customs duties or tolls, and so the gates or ports by which merchandise entered or left the burgh were important features. There were ports in the north, south, east and western edges of the burgh. Tolls were collected at these ports by designated officers, or custumerii. The ports were also used to display limbs of executed criminals, as a macabre deterrent to other would-be miscreants. At times of plague the ports were filled up with turfs to stop infected people getting into the town.

The West Port spanned the High Street at about No 291. It was demolished secretly on the night of 14 July 1783 when one Frances Russell found it to be in the way of an addition to his house, West Park. The matter

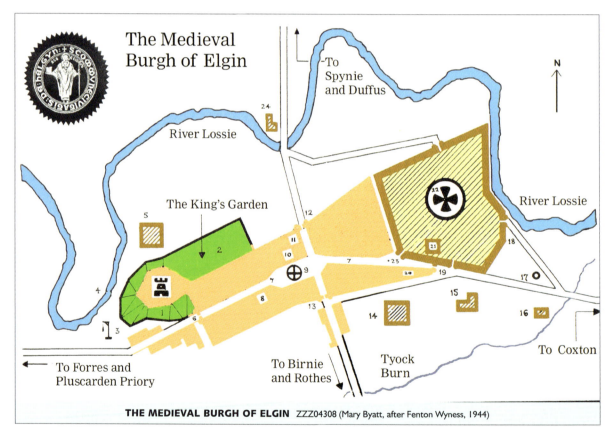

THE MEDIEVAL BURGH OF ELGIN ZZZ04308 (Mary Byatt, after Fenton Wyness, 1944)

1. The Castle, now Ladyhill. 2. The King's Garden. 3. Gallows Green. 4. Hangman's Ford. 5. Blackfriars' Monastery. 6. West Port. 7. The High Street. 8. Thunderton House. 9. Tolbooth, St Giles Kirk and Market Cross. 10. Preceptory of the Knights Templar. 11. Commandery of the Knights Hospitaller of St John. 12. North Port. 13. South Port. 14. Greyfriars' Monastery. 15. Maison Dieu. 16. Leper's House. 17. Order Pot. 18. East Port. 19. Bede House. 20. The Brethren of St Lazarus. 21. The Cathedral. 22. The Little Cross. 23. The Bishop's Mill.

was hushed up, and he escaped prosecution. The North Port, halfway down Lossie Wynd, was taken down legally in 1787; a plaque on the wall of a house marks its former position. The East Port near the Bede Houses was also taken down at the end of the 18th century, but Elgin's South Port (Smithy Port), near the crossroads at the top of Moss Street, remained in existence for another hundred years, and was removed as late as 1892.

By about 1400, Elgin had attained effective self-government. The population had increased to some 1,500 souls, and the greatly enhanced prosperity of the merchants and craftsmen was reflected in the more substantial buildings that fronted the High Street. The houses were now arranged gable to gable, with a 'pend' or archway to one side, leading through to the backlands, or tofts, that burghers used for their trade or as small crofts. The pend would have been secured at night by a strong yett (door).

In time the population grew still further, and a single line of houses was built down the west side of each toft, at right angles to the High Street, and so closes were formed. Houses in a close all had their doors and windows facing east, so that neighbours had some privacy, and they were graded in size from the High Street outwards, with larger ones at the High Street end. To the south, beyond the backlands, there were now crofts extending down to the marshlands known today as the Wards. To the north was common land known as the Town's Crofts (Burgh or Borough Briggs). It is still common ground to this day.

The Town Drummer

The Town Drummer was responsible for timekeeping within the burgh. The first drummer to be mentioned by name was Magnus Edmonstone, who held the post from 1625 to 1633. His duties were to make rounds of the town at 4am and 5am, beating the town drum all the while. The church bell was rung an hour later at 6am. At the end of the day the church bell was rung at 8pm, and at 9pm the Town Drummer made his final round. In 1706 the evening curfew was moved to 10pm, 'a fitter hour for tradesmen to leave off their work'. In the 1760s William Edward became Town Drummer, and held the post for 60 years at a salary of £24 Scots per annum. When the Poet Laureate, Robert Southey, visited Elgin in 1819, he complained about '... an abominable drum ... beaten at nine'. William Edward died in 1822, and was succeeded by his son of the same name.

THE TOWN DRUM IN THE ELGIN MUSEUM 2005
ZZZ04309 (Mary Byatt)

THE HIGH STREET

The central part of the town was built around the old church of St Giles with its graveyard and market cross. Graveyards were the places where people met to exchange goods and where announcements were made - hence their association with market crosses. They later became the places where tolls were levied and justice was carried out.

THE CROSSES

Ancient crosses marked the sites of markets. The Little Cross at the east end of the High Street may have been used as a mercat cross for a separate settlement dependent on the cathedral, as in Aberdeen, but documentation is lacking. Built where the cathedral sanctuary wall abutted the town, the original cross on this site was probably funded by Alexander Macdonald, 3rd son of the Lord of the Isles, who 'spulzied' the cathedral and chanonry in 1402 and, when punished, gave a sum of gold for 'a cross & bell'. The current Little Cross was erected towards the end of the 16th century, and became the site of public scourging and use of the jougs (a metal band that was locked around the neck to restrain a person). By 1867 the whole structure had fallen into disrepair. The sundial and finial were so worn that they were removed and replaced by a facsimile. The originals were put in the museum next door.

The first mention of the market cross of the Burgh of Elgin was in 1365, and it probably stood within the graveyard of St Giles's Church. By 1630, an elaborate

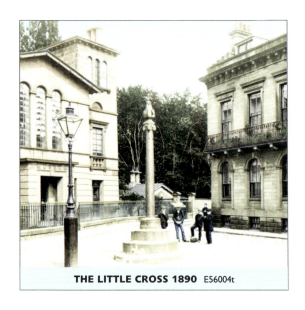

THE LITTLE CROSS 1890 E56004t

THE LITTLE CROSS, EAST END OF THE HIGH STREET c1935 EM00010 (The Elgin Museum)

mercat cross stood on the site of the current Muckle Cross, remaining there from the reign of Charles I until 1792, when it was taken down. The present cross is a copy by Sidney Mitchell, and was erected in 1888. Only the lion on the top of the column survives from the previous cross. The large hexagonal tower at the base of the column has an internal stairway. The platform at the top of this stairway used to be used for royal proclamations, but is now said to be unsafe.

The following description of Elgin's High Street in 1798, from 'A Survey of the Province of Moray', is interesting but not very complimentary: 'The town consists of one principal street, in a winding course, for little more than a mile from east to west, widened to such breadth towards the middle of the town as to have the church awkwardly placed upon it, and at a distance farther on, the town-house, a mean building, adjoined to a clumsy square tower, almost without windows, which contains the hall where the courts and county meetings are held, and the common gaol.' The writer goes on to say that the parish church was 'a low clumsy misshapen building, at once deforming and incumbering the street'.

THE PROCLAMATION OF THE ACCESSION OF EDWARD VIII 1937
ZZZ04337 (Reproduced by kind permission of the Editor, The Northern Scot)

At this date the platform of the Muckle Cross was still being used for announcements.

OLD ST GILES FROM THE WEST 1839
ZZZ04310 (Author's Collection)

Old St Giles was indeed a church of more character than elegance, but it was respected for being the first church in Elgin, founded between 1180 and 1200, well before the cathedral was built. It was constructed in a severe Gothic cruciform shape, with un-aisled choir and transepts, a low central tower, and an aisled nave of five bays. The roof was covered with huge heavy stones instead of slate, and was supported by two rows of massive pillars. Side altars were funded by the various trades, but were abolished at the time of the Reformation. In their place, lofts or galleries were constructed, and each trade had its own area where its members sat. The front of each loft was beautifully carved with the arms and motto of the respective craft. The shield from the loft of the hammermen (metalsmiths) can be seen in the museum.

Such was the anti-papist sentiment after the Reformation that the 'papist' bells were sent to Turriff to be recast into 'one solid, sound Presbyterian bell'. The Prayer Bell (or

A CARVED SHIELD OF THE HAMMERMEN 2005
ZZZ04311 (Mary Byatt)

The shield was originally placed at the front of the hammermen's loft in St Giles's Church. It is now in the Elgin Museum.

Minister's Bell) survived unscathed, and is said to bear the pre-Reformation inscription 'Thomas de Dunbar me fecit, 1402'.

In the late 16th and 17th century Episcopacy

and Presbyterianism struggled for supremacy. When St Giles's was Episcopalian, there was a bishop, and when Presbyterian there was a General Assembly. There were at least six changes between 1563 and 1688.

Over the years further structural changes took place within the church. In 1621 the arch separating the nave and the chancel was walled up, creating two churches - the Little Kirk to the east and the Muckle Kirk to the west. The Little Kirk was used for Episcopalian services and the Muckle Kirk for Presbyterian services. The Muckle Kirk's roof collapsed in 1679 and cost £4,000 Scots to repair, the money being raised by public subscription from a population now numbering some 3,000. In the early years of the 18th century, the Muckle Kirk's north and south aisles were removed to allow widening of the High Street. In 1753 the inside walls were plastered for the first time. The Little Kirk fell into disrepair, and was demolished in 1800; the stone was used to construct a new school in Academy Street.

The Muckle Kirk was a large church capable of housing 2,000 people, and it was greatly revered. The interior was lit by the light of hundreds of candles in huge brass chandeliers, which was said to be a sight not to be forgotten. There was general dismay at the proposal in 1826 'to sweep it utterly away', and to replace it with something grander and more modern. The sturdy columns and arches were in good order, but the roof timbers were probably rotten, and the church was demolished because another collapse was feared. The demolition in 1826 was

said to 'fill the street with the remains of the dead ... Large quantities of bones were carried away, showing the extent of interment within the old church.' All that remains of the old Muckle Kirk today are its two bells, its communion plate in the new church, and its old pulpit dated 1694, now in St Columba's Church in Moss Street.

The other building referred to by the writer of 'A Survey of the Province of Moray' (1798) was the tolbooth. The name 'tolbooth' was derived from its function as a booth where goods were weighed and tolls were levied. There are no drawings of the early tolbooth, but it was said to be an insecure wooden booth from which imprisoned debtors often escaped. A more secure tolbooth was built in 1605 using stones taken from the churchyard of St Giles's. Then in 1701, this new tolbooth was burnt down by a prisoner, Robert Gibson of Linkwood 'in his furiosity'. A replacement tolbooth was started in 1709 and finished six years later at a cost of £4,000 Scots. The contractors upheld an old superstition that was supposed to guarantee them a thriving future: they did not pay the workmen their last week's wages. For this they became the tolbooth's first prisoners.

The Elgin Tolbooth now consisted of a council chamber to the west and a prison tower to the east. Underneath the council chamber were four vaulted apartments, one of which was 'the black hole' where petty delinquents were confined for 12 to 24 hours at a time. Another was let to a cooper, who is said to have made a terrible noise at his work making barrels. The prison tower had five

THE TOLBOOTH AND THE HIGH STREET IN 1820
ZZZ04312 (An old print from H B Mackintosh, 1914)

The cooper who can be seen at the front of the tolbooth is said to have disturbed the Town Council with his hammering.

vaulted apartments, one on top of the other, reached by an extruding stair. The ground floor was the military guardhouse, the first floor was the clerk's office, the second floor was the debtors' prison, and the third floor was for criminals. Here felons were fettered to an immense iron bar that is now in the Elgin Museum. There was no fireplace and no glass in the small windows, the aim being to make wrong doers more frightened of the discomfort of the prison than of the magistrates. The top floor of the tower was used for civil prisoners; the bartizan (the battlemented parapet) provided a walkway

around which debtors and lesser criminals could take exercise. Up here was the common latrine, a wooden box that was emptied into the street once a week. An outside mealhouse was attached to the prison and dispensed meal to the starving at times of poor harvests.

The Tolbooth was taken down in 1843 and its stones sold to the builders of the Free Church. At the Moray Mechanic's Society dinner on 17 October that year, a song was sung dedicated to the memory of the tolbooth. One verse of that song ran:

'The big bell that once gart the toon
   luik sae braw,
Rang in generations and cheer'd them awa',
   In days o' rejoicing, wi' puing an' hoizing,
'Twas a wonder its sullen sides gaedna in
   twa.
Its tongue was no stranger in moments o'
   danger,
The Grants o' Strathspey had nae reason to
   craw,
The cock saw them comin', the bell set
   a-bummin',
Till the rievers grew heartless, an' hurrit
   awa'.

The big bell that the song refers to was cast in 1712 by Albert Gelly, who worked in Forsyth's Close. It is now in the Elgin Museum.

In addition to being locked up in the tolbooth, an earlier form of punishment was to be thrown in the Order Pot, a deep pool left by an old course of the river Lossie, used for trial by ordeal. It was so deep that it was believed to be bottomless. The use of deep pools for punishment was mentioned in an act of Parliament in 1567. The act laid down punishments for specific offences. 'For the third fault (fornication) [the offender was] to be taken to the deepest and foulest pule of water of the town or parish, there to be thrice douket and thereafter to be banished the said town or parish for ever'. Many so-called witches suffered a similar fate.

The Punishment of Witches

After the Reformation, the attitude to witchcraft changed from sufferance to intolerance. No longer was it permissible to placate witches' 'evil' spirits by putting oatmeal out for them. These poor souls were often no more than local herbalists, and one such was Marjory Bisset, who in 1560 was dragged to the Order Pot by a large crowd and was accused by a leper of giving him ointment that had withered his arm. *'The people did press round and become clamorus, and they take the woman and drag her, amid many tears and cryes, to the pool, and crie 'To tryal, to tryal', and soe they plonge her into the water. An quwhen, as she went down in the water, ther was ane gret shoute, but as she rose again, and raised up her armes, as gif she wode have come up, there was silence for ane space, when agane she went doune with ane bubbling noise, they shouted finallie 'To Sathan's Kyngdom she hath gone', and forthwith went their wayes.'*

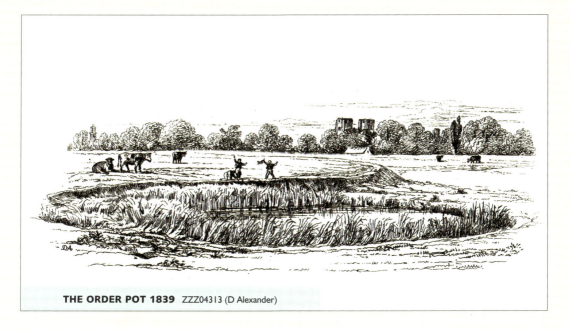

THE ORDER POT 1839 ZZZ04313 (D Alexander)

The order pot became the town's first landfill site, and after receiving all the rubbish from the damaged cathedral and the foundations of the Muckle Kirk, it was eventually filled in with silt from the Tyock burn when the burn was dredged in 1881. A stone marking the site of the Order Pot was erected by the Town Council in 1893, and can be seen on the grass to the north side of the A96 beside Tyock Industrial Estate.

THE WYNDS AND CLOSES

In time, two new streets were added to Elgin parallel to the High Street, one to the north and one to the south. They were known as the North Back Gait and the South Back Gait. They ran along the ends of the burghers' backlands, and were linked to the High Street by wynds and closes. The writer of 'A Survey of the Province of Moray' describes the town in 1798 thus: 'Behind the houses which front the street, buildings are carried back on either side, in narrow lanes, for the length of eight or ten dwellings, in some cases separate properties, and containing for the most part distinct families. Many of these lanes terminate in the gardens, affording more immediate access to the country than the few public avenues offer.'

Some of the lanes referred to were wider and were known as wynds. Only the names Lossie Wynd (once Shambles Wynd) and Murdoch's Wynd remain to this day; others have been renamed: the street now called Commerce Street was once School Wynd, and the Cathedral Road was Wiseman's Wynd. South Back Gait has become South Street, and North Back Gait all but disappeared when the

inner ring road was built in 1973. Closes were often named after the family that lived there or after some craft carried on in the Backlands. Thus Glover Street, beside the council offices, was once Glovers Close, where gloves were made. Many of the picturesque names of the closes were discarded when the High Street houses were numbered.

Writing in The Elgin Courant and Courier of 25 December 1938, an Elgin citizen, Charles Archibald, gave a vivid and somewhat nostalgic account of the closes in his early childhood, sixty years before. He described each close as having its own customs and atmosphere. In some, he says, 'brave attempts were made to conceal their state of indigence, to hold the head high and to maintain what was, after all, but a grim appearance of respectability. Other closes almost flaunted their filth and their rags, their drunkenness, their immorality, their idleness.' But the majority 'adopted the middle course, being neither eminently clean nor rigidly respectable'. The slum district was at the foot of Ladyhill, and it was here that the Moray author Jessie Kesson (1916-1994) spent her childhood in one of the closes.

So life in the closes did not conform to the picturesque image one would like to hold of them from the few that remain today. The houses were usually damp, gloomy and overcrowded. An article in The Elgin Courant of 11 October 1912 referred to them as 'old, very old, and small and pokey. You stoop to enter, climb tortuous stairs and find yourself in wee boxes o' places. A room and a bed closet with perhaps a coal cellar under a stair comprises the accommodation for a married couple and a small family.'

But the social life of the closes was much missed by old folks who were later moved out into better accommodation on the perimeter of the town. They complained that they could no longer walk up to the High Street and 'have a news'. As late as 1946, parts of the old garden walls beyond the closes were a common sight, but few remain today. The closes themselves were still cobbled, and their common drains or sewers were still visible along the east side against the back wall of the neighbouring close.

SOME OLD HIGH STREET BUILDINGS

The oldest house in the High Street is Thunderton House. It was originally known as the Great Lodging or King's House, and was used by visiting royalty from the late 14th century onwards. At one time it was a huge courtyard palace surrounded by gardens and orchards that extended from the High Street to South Street. The original charter was granted to Thomas Randolph by his uncle, King Robert the Bruce. In 1455 the property passed by forfeiture to the Dunbars of Westfield. Some time after 1603 it was back in the hands of the Earls of Moray, and it was then sold in 1650 to the Sutherlands of Duffus. Lord Duffus enlarged it and added a squat tower with a bartizan. He placed a carving of an immense stone savage on each side of the tower's main entrance. They had pointed beards and hair in the style of Charles I, and were said to represent the supporters of his coat of arms.

In 1746, Thunderton House was occupied by a noted Jacobite, Mrs Anderson of Arradoul (known as 'Lady Arradoul'). Prince Charles Edward Stuart was said to have stayed here with 'an inflammatory cold' for some days before the battle of Culloden. Lady Arradoul kept the prince's sheets and requested in her will that she be buried in them. In 1800 the property was bought by Mr John Batchen, an auctioneer, who altered it extensively. He turned it into a mill and a preaching house, and feued the eastern part, forming Batchen Street. 'Mr Haldane's Church' was built on the High Street frontage. The squat tower was taken down in 1822 to make room for the construction of Batchen Lane; the two caryatid savages from its doorway lay for some time at Pluscarden Abbey before being moved to the Elgin Museum. Thunderton House is now an inn, and is hemmed in behind the Elgin Sweet Shop and Asher's bakery.

THUNDERTON HOUSE, AS ENLARGED BY LORD DUFFUS c1800 EM00011 (The Elgin Museum)

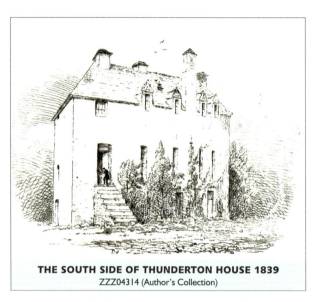

THE SOUTH SIDE OF THUNDERTON HOUSE 1839
ZZZ04314 (Author's Collection)

Here we see the house after the removal of the square tower.

THE SOUTH SIDE OF THUNDERTON HOUSE 2005
E56704k (Mary Byatt)

Note that stairs still lead to the original first floor entrance.

The building that is known as The Tower at 103 High Street is another very old building in Elgin's High Street. It has an extruding stair leading to principal rooms on the first floor, a common feature of houses of the late 17th and early 18th centuries. The Tower was built in 1634 by a merchant and magistrate, Alexander Leslie of Glen of Rothes, and is corbelled into a square at the top, like the towers at Ballindalloch Castle. There was once an iron cross of the Knights of Malta on top of it.

THE ARMS OF ALEXANDER LESLIE ON THE TOWER
ZZZ04315 (Mary Byatt)

Alexander Leslie built The Tower. His correct colours have been added to the drawing.

The property passed to David Stewart, Provost of Elgin, whose son represented the burgh in the Scottish parliament of 1699. Later it became the property of the Forsyth family, and from 1789 to his death, Isaac Forsyth ran a large bookselling business here. He also used it as a base for the north of Scotland's first circulating library.

An enterprising and energetic man, Isaac Forsyth was one of the founders of the Elgin Museum, and the secretary to the Morayshire Farmers Club. He was also the person responsible for employing John Shanks to clear up the cathedral ruins. The Tower was 'baronialised' in 1876 and used as the Tower Hotel. It is now owned by Ritsons, a firm of accountants, who use it for office space.

THE TOWER IN 2003   E56705k (Mary Byatt)

THE TOWER c1870   EM00012 (The Elgin Museum)

Alexander Leslie's arms are beside the first floor window.

The arcaded buildings for which Elgin is famous were not built until the 17th century, by which time the population had doubled to around 3,000. The houses were mostly three storeys high with the third storey breaking through the stone-slabbed roof in a row of richly ornamented dormers. The walls were harled, allowing use of cheaper stone. The gable ends were crow-stepped and had the lowest stone jutting out to form a skew-put. Both the dormers and skew-puts were ornamented with the owner's initials, the dates of construction, or a coat of arms. The ground floor had an open arcaded front made of well-tooled stone, and the lower rooms were set back from the street. Boswell recorded in 1797 that 'there was sometimes a walk for a considerable length under a cloister, which is now frequently broken because the new houses have another form, but seems to have been uniformly continued in the old city'. The rooms behind the arcades must have been rather gloomy. Nowadays the arches are filled in with glass to make shop windows, which seem very small compared to the huge plate-glass windows of neighbouring buildings. The style of the arcaded buildings is thought to have been imported from the continent during the period of sea trade with the Low Countries.

The distinctive arcaded houses survived until the beginning of the Victorian era, when they were destroyed to make way for bigger and better houses. Only three now remain, and all are at the east end of the High Street. Nos 44/46 (1688) and 50/52 (1694) on the south side are two fine examples, and their restoration in 1959 won a Civic Trust Award. The first of these buildings was the Red Lion Inn, at which Dr Johnson stayed in 1773. He wrote: 'About noon we came to Elgin, where, in the inn that we supposed the best, a dinner was set before us, which we could not eat. This was the first time, and except one, the last, that I found any reason to complain of a Scottish table.' Word has it that he was served a poor meal because he was mistaken by the waiter for one Thomas Pauter, a travelling merchant who came to the inn often and was known to prefer drink to food.

THE RED LION INN BUILDING 2005 E56706k (Mary Byatt)

The walkway under the arcade is now filled in with shop windows.

THE PEND LEADING TO RED LION CLOSE IN THE EARLY 20TH CENTURY EM00013 (The Elgin Museum)

Note the old paving.

Red Lion Close, which runs through the old Red Lion Inn building, is a good example of a surviving close. It used to house the stables for the Red Lion Inn, and afterwards Mr Jack's tallow candle factory - the candle factory ceased to be of use after gas was introduced to Elgin in 1830. The close has now been restored, and is paved.

The other fine example of an arcaded house is Braco's Banking House, which is on the north side of the High Street at No 7; it was carefully restored in 1975. Its roof is covered with the thick stone slabs once used throughout Elgin, and its decorated dormer windows are typical of the architecture of the time. This building was the town house of Innes of Coxton, and was built in 1694 for John Duncan and Margaret Innes. Their initials can be seen above the dormer windows, along with an Innes star. From 1703 to 1722, the house was owned by the banker William Duff of Dipple and Braco. He and his brother Alexander made a fortune by lending money on estates at the time of poor harvests and by taking possession of properties that had been advanced as security.

The writer Daniel Defoe visited Scotland several times around the time of the Union

THE PEND LEADING TO SHEPHERD'S CLOSE 2005 E56707k (Mary Byatt)

This close is next to 50/52 High Street; here we see the new paving.

of Parliaments in 1707. He found Elgin a congenial place, and wrote: 'As the country is rich and pleasant, so here are a great many rich inhabitants, and in the town of Elgin in particular, for the gentlemen, as if this were Edinburgh or the Court for this part of the Island, leave their Highland habitations in winter and come and live for the diversion of the place, and plenty of provisions; and there is, on this account, a great variety of gentlemen for society. This makes Elgin a very agreeable place to live in'. So on the High Street at this time there were several town houses owned by lairds of Moray, who used them mainly in winter.

The only remaining 18th-century houses are at the east end of the High Street, on the north side. The Kilmolymock Masonic Lodge at No 17 High Street is one of them; it has an unusual Venetian window, dated around 1750. Restoration of these buildings was one of the first projects of the Elgin Fund in the late 1960s.

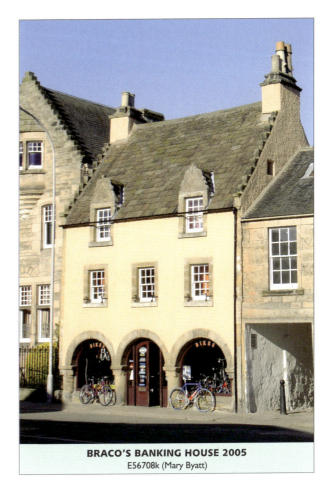

BRACO'S BANKING HOUSE 2005
E56708k (Mary Byatt)

MARKETS

In the 16th century there were six livestock fairs a year, based on the church calendar: Fastern's E'en, in February just before Lent; Pasch at Easter; Trinity Tide one week after Whitsun; St Giles on 1 September; Michaelmas on 29 September; and Andersmass on 30 November. They were held on land to the west of Elgin at Bruceland, and merchants were attracted from far and wide. Later, the dates of cattle markets were changed to a more regular timetable for convenience. As well as these large cattle markets, there would have been smaller, weekly markets, based on the graveyard of St Giles's. The Plainstones to the west of St Giles's Kirk were laid out in 1787 as an open exchange where fisherfolk from the coast could bring their fish for sale.

The weekly market was not brought under cover until 1851, when a covered market on the south side of the High Street at No 130 was opened. 'The New Market has proved a most humane blessing to the whole community, but in a particular manner to the fisherwomen who had to sit or stand near the Cross, exposed to all sorts of weather - a most pitiful spectacle in a town where all else was pleasant.' (Lachlan Mackintosh, 1891). The site stretched right through from the High Street to South Street, where there was a grand arched entrance bearing a mask of Bacchus. The market has disappeared, and the site is now a bar and nightclub called The Jailhouse on the High Street side and a More store on the South Street side.

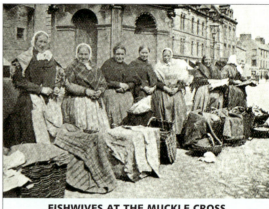

FISHWIVES AT THE MUCKLE CROSS
ZZZ04316 (Reproduced by kind permission of the editor,
The Northern Scot)

THE HIGH STREET ENTRANCE TO THE 1851 NEW MARKET 2005 E56709k (Mary Byatt)

The space behind is now used for bars and clubs.

WELLS

The only well still in use is Marywell at the foot of Ladyhill. It is said to have supplied holy water to the chapel dedicated to the Blessed Virgin Mary within the castle on the hill above it. Legend has it that its water is colder and denser in summer than in winter.

Elgin had three town wells, supplemented by wells within some of the closes. The best water was said to have come from the Little Cross Well, which was the last of Elgin's three town wells to be used. It was built around 1644 and was 32 feet deep, with water 5 feet deep. It remained open until 1811, when it was covered and had a pump put in it. The old wooden pump was replaced with a metal one in 1834. Water was supplied to the town by gravitation in 1840, but the Little Cross well continued to be used in times of emergency. The site of the well is now marked by a plaque on the wall of Somerfield supermarket.

MILLS

The river Lossie that runs through Elgin has driven many mills over the centuries. Oldmills was the first mill of Elgin, or King's Mill, until 1230; then Alexander II bestowed it on the monks at Pluscarden, so giving the multures (dues) to the monks. This annoyed the burghers of Elgin, and a convention was held in 1272 in the kirkyard of St Giles's between them and the monks of Pluscarden. Somehow the issue was settled, but in 1330, disputes arose over payment of the dues; these continued on down the centuries until the dues were finally abolished in 1818. After that, the inhabitants of Elgin were allowed to grind their own corn in a mill of their choice. The Earl of Fife, to whom the multures were paid at that time, was given £635 compensation, with which he bought the fields to the west and south of Dr Gray's. Although originally a meal mill, Oldmills also served as a brewery in the 17th century.

OLDMILLS IN 2003   E56710k (Mary Byatt)

The second of Elgin's mills was at Bishopmill, and was probably built in 1203 when Bishop Bricius arrived at Spynie. By 1309 the mill had two grinding wheels, and both oatmeal and flour were milled there. It was one of many buildings burnt down by Montrose in 1645. Slezer's engraving,

'Prospect of the Town of Elgin' (1693), shows the restored mill to the right. Beside it is a fulling mill where cloth was shrunk and thickened. A dye house was added in 1716. The mill on the left of Slezer's engraving is Deanshaugh Mill.

SLEZER'S 'PROSPECT OF THE TOWN OF ELGIN'
1693 EM00014 (The Elgin Museum)

In 1237, Bishop Andrew Moray granted land for a mill at Sheriffmill to his kinsman, Walter de Moravia, on condition that he gave him 'a reddendo of a pound of pepper and the same quantity of cumin seed' every year. The mill remained in the hands of the church until the Reformation, and then passed to the Duffus family. Nothing remains of it now, but the name has stayed on in the form of a bridge. Just upstream of Sheriffmill is Scroggiemill, another very old corn mill. Downstream of Oldmills is Deanshaugh; here there was a tobacco mill, a waulk mill, a flax mill and bleaching machinery, all of which were later replaced by a sawmill. At Kingsmill there were meal and wood mills, and at Linkwood another waulk mill, where cloth was 'walked' to combine the warp and the weft and so thicken it. Newmill, near the cathedral, was taken over by James Johnston in 1800, and its corn mill was converted to a wool mill.

CRAFTS

In the 17th century Elgin became increasingly prosperous. Research has indicated that this prosperity was due more to the skills of its craftsmen than to the ability of its burghers to trade. Between 1540 and 1660, there appears to have been a predominance of skinners, with tanners, cordiners, glovers and saddlers much in evidence too. Not only were leather workers the most numerous, they were also the wealthiest of the craftsmen. There was a wealth hierarchy of crafts, from skinners, glovers and litsters (dyers) at the top to baxters (bakers) and brewers at the bottom. The most successful craftsmen were those who made use of local resources and either found a market outside the burgh or a lucrative market within. The source of leather would have been the fine cattle reared on the rich, fertile land of the Laich of Moray and its hinterland. Cattle were slaughtered in the shambles at the bottom of Lossie Wynd. The relatively small volume of overseas trade led to a parity of wealth between the merchants and some of the wealthier craftsmen, unlike Aberdeen, where merchants were the more prosperous. In Elgin there were no distinct social units, and marriage between relatives of craftsmen and of merchants was common.

TRADE

There is evidence of foreign trade through the bishops' harbour at Spynie as early as 1234, and ships were still coming into this port in 1400. After that, the silting up of the loch stopped the entry of deep draft ships. Loch Spynie eventually lost its connection

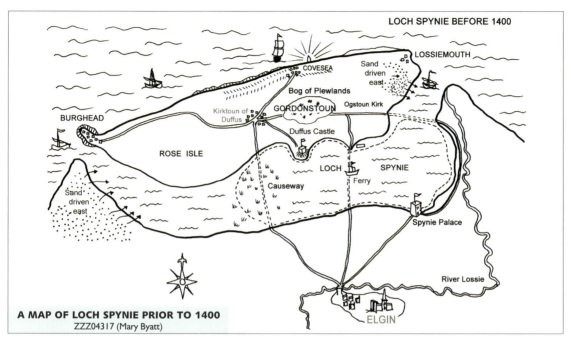

A MAP OF LOCH SPYNIE PRIOR TO 1400
ZZZ04317 (Mary Byatt)

A safe harbour before it silted up, Loch Spynie must have been largely responsible for the importance of Elgin.

to the sea and became an inland loch. In 1393, the Earl of Moray granted the burghers of Elgin freedom from customs on goods exported through his harbour at the mouth of the Spey. Malt, salted fish, wool and cloth were shipped out to continental Europe in exchange for silk, wine and ironware. The fine 14th-century Flemish flagon found in an Elgin close is evidence of early trade with Flanders. It is now in the museum.

At one time Elgin had a flourishing trade in ale; indeed, there were 80 private brewers in Elgin in 1687. The principal innkeeper, William Douglas, is said to have brewed 4,000 gallons of ale and 400 gallons of aqua vitae in three months. Some of this was exported to Holland, Norway and the Baltic states. The trade in ale flourished until 1707, when it was killed off by the imposition of a tax of 2p

Scots per pint of ale. As the trade in ale waned, so the tax that was collected from it fell, but sufficient revenue was raised in the first three years of the tax to complete the building of the west pier in Lossiemouth. Trade in grain then took the place of trade in ale, grain being sent down by ship to Leith and to London.

An increase in trade in fine linen also followed the demise of the trade in ale. Lint was grown and spun in the Laich of Moray and woven into table and bed linen and fine cambric for church

THE ARMS OF THE EARL OF MORAY ZZZ04318
(Mary Byatt)

The 'three cushions lozengeways' are really three woolsacks.

dignitaries. People called the Stampers were responsible for quality control. They inspected the cloth and marked it 'stamped in Elgin'. In 1748, the Trustees for the Encouragement of the Linen Manufacturers of North Britain offered prizes for certain kinds of linen. By 1788 it was recorded that some 55,000 yards of linen were stamped, bringing in some £3,500. At one time the value of the combined production of linen cloth and thread by Huntly, Banff, Elgin and Forres was £125,000 annually.

The earliest references to the hammermen (metal workers) are from the 16th century, at which time Elgin was one of very few centres in the north for goldsmiths and silversmiths. The 1686 carved wooden crest of the hammermen from St Giles's Kirk is in the museum. Elgin silver is much sought after by collectors. Marks are ELGIN, ELGN or ELG, and sometimes the twin towers of the west front of the cathedral. A particularly fine piece of Elgin silver is the snuffbox presented to John Shanks when he became too feeble to continue working in the cathedral ruins. This was made by W S Ferguson of Elgin and has an engraving of the west end of the cathedral on one side and a tribute to John Shanks on the reverse side. It is on display in the museum.

JOHN SHANK'S SNUFFBOX 2005
ZZZ04319 (Mary Byatt)

TRADE CORPORATIONS

Here and there in the stonework of Elgin's old houses and the tombs in the Cathedral you can see the marks of the Trades. Trade corporations formalising the crafts of the town were set up in the middle of the 17th century, by which time the population of Elgin numbered some 2,500. There were at first six trade corporations - weavers, tailors, glovers, shoemakers, hammermen and wrights. Fleshers were added later. Each Trade had its own Deacon and a Boxmaster, who were elected by the council. The Boxmaster looked after the chest containing the important documents and money of his Trade. The weavers' box can be seen in the museum. The six Deacons were elected

> ## Did you know?
>
> *In 1687 there were 80 private brewers in Elgin, and the principal publican brewed 4,000 gallons of ale in three months. The east and west piers at Lossiemouth were largely built with the revenue from tax imposed on ale in Elgin.*

Did you know?

Names of Trades

Builders were called wrights

Metalworkers or metal smiths were called hammermen

Weavers were websters

Shoemakers were cordiners or souters

Bakers were called baxters

Butchers were fleshers

Dyers were called litsters

annually, and the Town Council chose one of them as Deacon Convener. He became one of the main officers of the Town Council, along with the Provost, Bailies and Dean of Guild. The Trades were controlled by the Town Council, and were permitted to exercise their respective handicrafts and to have employees and apprentices. From 1705 the Trades were allowed to elect their own Deacons and Boxmasters, but they were never allowed to encroach on the preserves of the Guildry Merchants, from whom they had to purchase all the raw materials of their craft. The Trade Corporations continued until after the Reform Bill in 1833, when an act was passed abolishing their exclusive privileges. They continued as Friendly Societies for the benefit of their members.

COMMUNICATION

Throughout the 18th century Elgin had little contact with the rest of Britain, except by sea. In 1798, there was a daily post runner from Elgin to Lossiemouth, but that was still the only regular contact with the outside world.

THE END OF THE 18TH CENTURY

The 18th century seems to have ended on a sad note. Boswell wrote that Elgin was 'a place of little trade and thinly inhabited'. Robert Young recorded in 'The Annals of the Parish and Burgh of Elgin' that 'the eighteenth century was not generally one of great progress in Scotland and like the preceding century it closed with a season of severe scarcity, almost approaching a famine. In the Burgh of Elgin, the Trade which had been so brisk and prosperous before the Union with England (1707) gradually declined and by the middle of the century the foreign trade, which consisted of exports of corn, malt, salmon and other home articles and the imports of wines, spirits, silk, hardware etc had entirely ceased, the fiscal laws of England having been extended to Scotland. This was succeeded by a demoralising contraband trade which long prevailed on the coast and in which many persons were largely engaged. There were few good homes erected in the Burgh during this century. Many of the old families left the town, and for the last fifty years the population seriously declined. In short, it was a time melancholy and depression.' Colonel Thomas Thornton (1784) had said that Elgin 'in filthiness exceeded all the towns of the north east'. All this was to change in the next century; by 1885 'a cleaner state of matter could not be found anywhere in the country'.

CHAPTER THREE

*The Age of Expansion -
1800 to 1899*

CONDITIONS IN ELGIN were not noticeably better in the early years of the 19th century than they had been in the final years of the previous century. Though Elgin had some fine houses in its centre, those at the east and west ends of the High Street, and in the closes, were still thatched and somewhat squalid. In 1819 the Poet Laureate, Robert Southey, visited Elgin and commented upon 'the appearance of decay'. It was many years before the filth in the closes and lanes was finally cleared up and stone privies built in the closes.

The ancient High Street had a row of huge blocks along its centre, referred to as the 'croon'. It was said to have been put there by Cromwell's men. On wet days people used these blocks as stepping-stones to keep out of the filth.

'Its causeway ha a 'croon'
For proud an' haughty feet Sir!'
(William Hay)

The street sloped away on each side to an open drain, and was crossed by two common gutters that ran south to north down to the river Lossie. The largest of the common gutters was beside the present Royal Bank of Scotland, and the second, smaller one, was near Shambles Wynd (Lossie Wynd). These gutters conveyed filthy water from the High Street down to Burgh Briggs and thence to the river Lossie.

In 1820, Provost Innes determined to rid the town of this nuisance and raised money to level the High Street, remove the 'croon',

Did you know?

Until 1820, Elgin's High Street had open sewers running along each side of it. The common gutters were much dreaded by drivers of coaches and post-chaises, whose wheels and springs were often broken as they rode over them.

place side pavements over the open drains, and put the common gutters in drains below the ground. The provost used to boast that he had 'paved the streets with 1000 guineas' (the cost of the project).

BENEFACTORS

Elgin's grandest buildings came into being early on in the 19th century as a result of generous bequests from two major benefactors. The buildings were not paid for out of proceeds of local trade, but rather by fortunes made in India by two sons of Elgin. Both of them worked for the Honourable East India Company. The first of these benefactors was Alexander Gray, son of a burgess of Elgin, who was a wheelwright and a watchmaker. The family home was in White Horse Inn Close, near Thunderton House. Alexander followed his mother's side of the family into the medical profession and qualified as a doctor in Edinburgh. In 1780 he was appointed assistant surgeon in the service of the East India Company. He made his fortune in Calcutta, died in 1807, and left £20,000 for a hospital 'for the sick of the poor in the town and county of Elgin'.

His framed will hangs in the hallway of the hospital. He bequeathed smaller sums of money to various relatives, but left only the interest from £7,000 to his 'most abandoned and deliberately infamous wife that ever distinguished the annals of turpitude, as proved by her letters and conduct'.

The foundation stone of Gray's Hospital was laid in 1815, the very day that news of victory at Waterloo reached Elgin. The hospital, designed by Gillespie Graham, and built at a cost of £6,000, was said to have 'wards full of brightness, very clean and orderly, the patients at peace. Even the very air is invigorating, sweeping in as it does, crisp and cool, from the North Sea only six miles away'. Graham made sure that the new hospital was imposing by piling all the facilities on top of one another in three storeys. Physicians, the matron and the dispensary were all on the ground floor, wards were on the first floor (males to the north and females to the south), and fever and smallpox patients were on the second floor.

The second of the two great benefactors was General Anderson (1745-1824). Son of a soldier, he was born abroad and was just an infant when his father died. His widowed mother brought her baby back to Elgin in 1747.

DR GRAY'S HOSPITAL 1880 SA000200 (Courtesy of University of St Andrews Library)

Note the single path up to the door.

Did you know?

General Anderson's widowed and impoverished mother took up residence in the ruins of the cathedral. She lived in the priest's room off the chapter house and used the stone hand basin (piscina) as a cradle for her infant son.

to the top of Ladyhill is by stone steps leading up between the arcades of the First World War memorial garden.

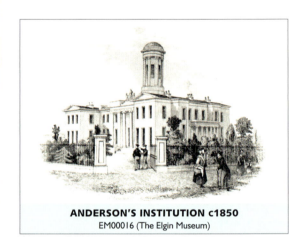

ANDERSON'S INSTITUTION c1850
EM00016 (The Elgin Museum)

Andrew Anderson was educated at Elgin's Grammar School in Commerce Street, and then left Moray to seek employment in London. On enlisting in the army, he was sent to serve in the East India Company, where he attained rank of Major General. When he died he left between £60,000 and £70,000 to the Sheriff and magistrates of Elgin to be used for the foundation of the Elgin Institution for the Support of Old Age and Education of Youth. The result was the building of Anderson's Institution on six acres of Maison Dieu land; it included a school and opened in 1832. The part used as a school was taken over in 1891 by the Burgh School Board and renamed East End School. When he was not in India, General Anderson's home in Elgin was a house on the site of the current Royal Bank of Scotland building.

There is no statue in Elgin commemorating either of these two generous benefactors. The prominent 80-foot Doric column on Ladyhill is topped by the fifth Duke of Gordon, a popular landowner who is said to have greatly improved the lot of his tenants. The column was constructed in 1839, and the figure was added a few years later. Access

LADYHILL AND THE DUKE OF GORDON'S MONUMENT 2005 E5671lk (Mary Byatt)

Dr Gray's Hospital and Anderson's Institution were both built in neo-classical style, with fine cut and polished stone facades. They were the start of the transformation of Elgin into a stately neo-classical town with a fine set of public buildings worthy of a regional capital. The rest of the town was still in a filthy state when they were built. The north side of the High Street alone had fifty-four dung heaps and twelve pigsties. Shambles Wynd, where livestock were slaughtered and butchered, had two open receptacles for dung and butchers' waste right on the edge of the Wynd.

POLITICS

Beneath the douce exterior of Elgin in the 19th century, political passions ran high. Rival parties were in direct and sometimes bloody confrontation. Mobs roamed the streets. In the general election of 1820, the Grant family supported Archibald Farquharson against the brother of the Earl of Fife. The Earl of Fife tried to bribe voters by handing out dresses, shawls, bonnets and pound notes on behalf of his brother. His supporters besieged Grant Lodge, home of the revered Lady Anne Grant. The fiery cross was raised up Speyside, and 700 Grant supporters rode on Elgin to raise the siege, where they were fed and were persuaded to go home. In another incident, Fife supporters kidnapped an Elgin bailie and transported him across the Moray Firth to Brora to prevent him voting in the election. The Grant representative won.

CHANGES IN THE TOWN PLAN

In the 1820s, the tight scale of the old medieval town plan was broached by the construction of Batchen Street and Commerce Street that connected the High Street to South Back Gait. North Street (1821) and a widened Lossie Wynd ran through to North Back Gait.

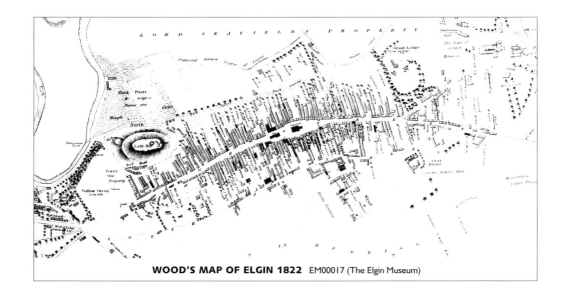

WOOD'S MAP OF ELGIN 1822 EM00017 (The Elgin Museum)

BURNS'S CENTENARY 1859 EM00018 (The Elgin Museum)

On 25 January 1859, the centenary of Robert Burns, great celebrations were held by Scots the world over. 'A picture was drawn of the High Street that day, with processions and bands of music, which will hand down to posterity the appearance of the town on that memorable occasion.'

The central part of the High Street was lined with three- or four-storey buildings for conduct of business, and the wealthy traders and businessmen now moved out to live in spacious villas to the south, all built using sandstone from quarries near the coast.

The first suburb of stone villas to be built was on land between Moss Street in the east and Dr Gray's Hospital in the west. Moray Street, Academy Street, Reidhaven Street and South Guildry Street were laid out here, and to this day are lined with attractive stone villas. New Elgin, with its single-storey stone buildings, was built as a workingman's suburb from 1830 onwards.

The small village of Bishopmill (now part of Elgin) had been laid out to the north of the river Lossie just before the turn of the

BISHOPMILL, THE DRY BRIG c1890 EM00019 (The Elgin Museum)

century. Its benefactor was the Earl of Findlater. As in Elgin, the Bishopmill High Street runs from east to west, and it still has some grand 19th-century houses on it. In 1820 a new road from Elgin to Lossiemouth was built through Bishopmill in a deep cutting that split its High Street in two. A 'dry bridge' was built over the new road to link the two halves of the High Street, but this 'Dry Brig' caused too much obstruction to traffic and was removed in 1898.

Demolition in 1822 of the derelict and haunted Calder mansion on the High Street made space for the construction of North Street. The magnificent Assembly Rooms, designed by William Burns of Edinburgh and London, were built on the corner of the High Street and North Street at a cost of £3,000. Funding was in part by public subscription and part by the Trinity Lodge of Freemasons. The photograph (taken around 1870) shows that the building had an immense Venetian window topped by a pediment. The Assembly Rooms were said to be 'for the nobility and gentry of the county and town'. Upstairs was a large ballroom with a sprung floor. One end had a raised platform for an orchestra, and at the other end the ballroom opened out into a supper room.

Calder House Ghost Stories

Calder House was built by Thomas Calder of Sheriff Miln in 1669. By the beginning of the 19th century it was uninhabited, and had become dilapidated and haunted. Screams of torment were heard coming from the house on dark winter's evenings. They were said to belong to any weary traveller who had been enticed in by a steaming cauldron of broth, and then tipped into it. 'Nelly Homeless' pattered about in another part of the house. She would knock, enter, and with a grim unearthly smile, beg for the return of her lungs and liver, pointing to a great gash in her chest. Her moans proclaimed the state of torment in which she would stay until her body was made whole again. The house was demolished in 1822.

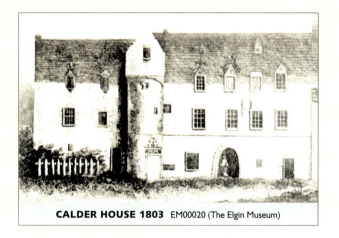

CALDER HOUSE 1803 EM00020 (The Elgin Museum)

Many grand and historic functions were held here, including a meeting of the gentry on 26 June 1837 to drink a toast to their new monarch, Queen Victoria.

THE ASSEMBLY ROOMS, THE BALLROOM IN THE EARLY 20TH CENTURY EM00021 (The Elgin Museum)

THE ASSEMBLY ROOMS (ON THE LEFT) c1870 EM00046 (The Elgin Museum)

The Muckle Spate

In 1829, six to nine inches of rain fell in the hills south of Elgin over a period of two days, producing the Great Flood of 4 August 1829. Sir Thomas Dick Lauder records in 'The Great Floods' that the mills and farm offices of Oldmills filled with water to within one foot of the door lintels. The area between Maryhill and Morriston braes was one mass of moving water, and houses beside the bridge at Bishopmill were inundated. Even the iron and the large bellows of a smith's forge here were carried off. Occupants of single-storey houses had to flee for their lives, whilst those who had little attics or small garrets roosted in them till the flood subsided. An immense stream ran up the road from Pansport and flooded the Maison Dieu lands as far as Ashgrove. On the lands of Pans there was a dry hillock that became a refuge for some horses. Later it was found to be covered with the dead and mutilated bodies of an immense number of moles, mice, rabbits, partridges, and hares that had gathered there for safety and had then been trampled on by the horses. When viewed from Ladyhill, Elgin resembled a city built on an island in the midst of an inland sea. Further north, the Lossie broke through into Loch Spynie, which became tidal again for a short while.

'STRANDED' c1830 ZZZ04320
(Sir Thomas Dick Lauder)

HIGH STREET 2005 E56712k (Mary Byatt)

This part of the High Street was once occupied by the Assembly Rooms. The Woolworth's building on the left was the Royal Bank of 1856.

Some years later, in 1856, the Royal Bank was built on the opposite corner of North Street. It was designed in Italianate style, with arched tops to the windows and a large cornice. The building still exists, and is now occupied by Woolworths. However, it is a sad fact that the much-admired Assembly Rooms were taken down in the 1960s, apparently condemned by dry rot.

In 1831 an outbreak of cholera brought great fear of infection, and was responsible for goading the town's authorities into finally cleaning up the streets. The 1833 Burgh Police Act provided the means of policing the state of cleanliness. In Elgin there were two police officers and two 'scavengers'. In 1842 a prison was built behind the courthouse, and a year later the tolbooth was demolished.

The work of the police officers was stretched to the limit by the meal riots of 1847. The potato harvest of 1846 had failed disastrously, and the price of meal had rocketed beyond the means of even the working poor. However, grain was still being exported in 1847 from Lossiemouth, Burghead and Findhorn. Rioting broke out, ships were raided, and grain was stolen. Law officers were injured, houses stoned, and effigies burnt. Troops were summoned, and the ringleaders were arrested and transported for 7 years.

A police office was added to the prison in 1851. The prison itself was enlarged in 1866, giving it 18 cells for criminals and 3 for debtors, plus accommodation for a prison governor and matron. The building no longer exists, and the police headquarters is now in Moray Street.

CHURCHES AND ARCHITECTS

Much of the character of Elgin is derived from its numerous churches. The new St Giles's Church, finished in 1828, is a fine neo-classical building, built at a cost of £8,700 by the architect Archibald Simpson of Aberdeen. It is in the form of a Greek Doric temple, and its tower is an imitation of the choragic monument in Athens that

HIGH STREET, ST GILES'S CHURCH c1899 SA000207
(Courtesy of University of St Andrews Library)

Lysicrates erected in honour of success in a choral competition. This large new church was a sign of Elgin's increasing prosperity in the early 19th century. It houses the two bells of its predecessor, the Muckle Bell and the Minister's Bell. The Muckle Bell was recast for the third time in 1785, and so is not very ancient; but the Minister's Bell, used to quieten the congregation when the minister enters, is over 500 years old.

Later churches were built in the Gothic revival style, and by 1908 there were a total of ten churches in Elgin. The architects that designed the new churches were usually local. One such was William Robertson (1786-1841), who was probably the north's first classical architect of substance. He was known and esteemed for his talents over the whole of the north of Scotland. His buildings in Elgin include the Scottish Episcopal Church of the Holy Trinity (1824), at the end of North Street, and the Elgin Court House (1838).

Robertson also built South Villa in Moss Street and Braemorriston House in Bishopmill, and he laid out King Street on the fringe of the former Chanonry in 1830. Robertson's architectural practice was carried on after his death by his nephews, A & W Reid, and then by J & W Wittet, who continue the practice to this day.

Following the Disruption of 1843, when many people left the established church, a plethora of new churches sprang up. Each was concerned to build a distinguished church of architectural merit. The first large church to be built was the High United Free Church in North Guildry Street (1843), with the

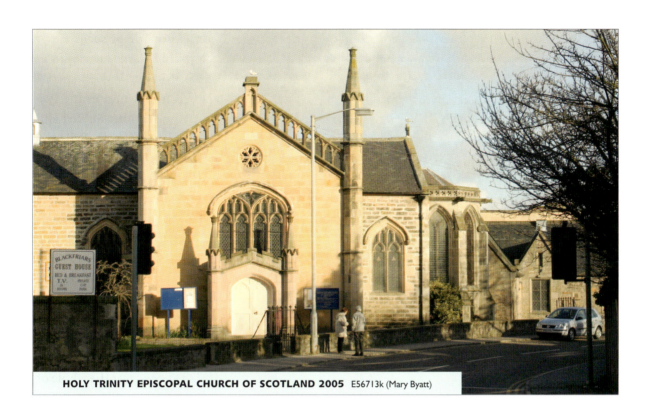

HOLY TRINITY EPISCOPAL CHURCH OF SCOTLAND 2005   E56713k (Mary Byatt)

popular Reverend Alexander Topp as its minister. He brought with him a congregation of 1,200 when he left the Church of Scotland. In 1850 the Baptist Church was built in Reidhaven Street. The popular High Church in North Guildry Street was soon too small for its growing congregation, and in 1852 A & W Reid built the United Free South Church in Moray Street to relieve it. Next they built the United Presbyterian Church in Moss Street (1858).

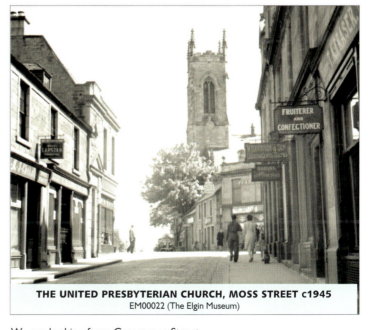

THE UNITED PRESBYTERIAN CHURCH, MOSS STREET c1945
EM00022 (The Elgin Museum)

We are looking from Commerce Street.

The dwindling of congregations in the 20th century has seen the closure of some of Elgin's fine churches. The Moss Street church was abandoned in 1938, and its congregation amalgamated with that of the South Church. In 1982 it became a soft furnishing store and in 1990 a restaurant, with its tower lowered after a stone from it had fallen through the roof of the bakery next door. The Evangelist's Hall in South Street, the one-time Salvation Army barracks, is now a second-hand furniture store, and the United Free South Church has been taken over as a nursery school.

A & W Reid were the most productive of all Elgin's Victorian architects, and their designs did not stop at churches. Following the laying out of Institution Road off Moss Street in 1830, they built most of the houses in it: Friars Park (1840), Kinrara (1850), Moray Bank (1850), and Friars House (1860). In the High Street, the Royal Bank (1856) and the Sheriff Court (1866) were also built to their design. In Commerce Street they built The Elgin Club (1868), a tall building in palazzo style, and the low building next to it, with a roofline of flat pediment, cornice, balustrade and urns - this is now the TSB. In Moray Street they built a new Academy (1885) - 'a temple of learning'. This is the fine classical building which lies in front of Moray College. In Duff Avenue they built The Lodge (1898) in an adventurous new American style.

THE SECOND ELGIN ACADEMY, BUILT IN 1801, NOW MORAY COLLEGE 2005 E56714k (Mary Byatt)

Another architect who put his stamp on Elgin was Thomas Mackenzie, who came to Elgin via Archibald Simpson's practice in Aberdeen. He designed the fountain on the Plainstones where the tolbooth once stood. It was built in 1846, three years after the tolbooth was demolished. It is of Grecian design, with three vases of diminishing size, arranged so that water cascades down from one vase to the next. The fountain was dry for many years in the 20th century and used as a planter, but the water supply was restored in 2003.

Thomas Mackenzie also built the Elgin Museum (1843), the Roman Catholic Church of Saint Sylvester at the head of Duff Avenue (1844), and the Station Hotel (1853), now the Laichmoray Hotel. The Roman Catholic Church has a beautiful Gothic gable facing down Duff Avenue, with fine tracery in its large window and an oculus above it.

From 1853 Thomas Mackenzie lived in Ladyhill House and enlarged it for himself. He is said to have built a loggia in the garden, incorporating carved stones that he collected from old Elgin buildings as they were demolished. After nineteen years of very prolific work, Thomas Mackenzie died of a fever aged only 40. His son, A Marshall Mackenzie, became an even more famous architect. As well as Marischal College in Aberdeen, one of his flamboyant buildings was the doomed Town Hall of 1885, on which he placed the weathercock from the old tolbooth.

SCHOOLS

Two of Elgin's earliest schools were the Grammar School (1489) and the Sang School (1594). Their buildings of 1694 and 1676 in School Wynd were combined in 1801 and replaced by the first Elgin Academy, at a cost of £505 12s 2d. The Academy was built at the top of the street now named Academy Street, and some of its buildings are still there. In 1886, the Academy moved to Moray Street, and was housed for some eighty years in A & W Reid's distinguished classical building. The modern Elgin Academy opened in 1969 on Morriston Road, and A & W Reid's

THOMAS MACKENZIE'S FOUNTAIN ON THE SITE OF THE OLD TOLBOOTH 2005 E56715k (Mary Byatt)

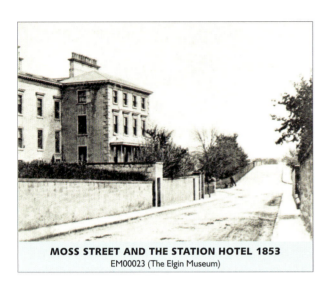

MOSS STREET AND THE STATION HOTEL 1853
EM00023 (The Elgin Museum)

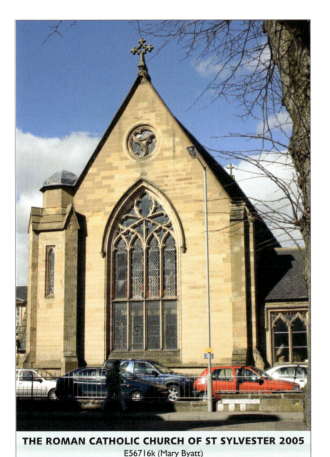

THE ROMAN CATHOLIC CHURCH OF ST SYLVESTER 2005
E56716k (Mary Byatt)

building became part of the college of further education.

In 1846, simmering discontent in the Town Council over the Church of Scotland's long-established authority over the Academy came to the boil. The presbytery took the council to court in order to confirm its right to govern the school. The Court of Session took 15 years to reach a decision, and, although the court found in favour of the presbytery on historical grounds, it was an empty victory. The Elgin Academy case changed the law of the land. An Act of Parliament of 1861 declared that 'no burgh school shall be subject to the government or discipline of the Established Church'.

As well as the Academy, Elgin had a wide diversity of other schools in the 19th century. The Trades School (1826-1874) was started by the six Incorporated Trades of Elgin, whose member craftsmen were mostly illiterate and wished to have their families educated. The fees of the Academy were beyond their means, so in 1826 they started a school of their own. They first used a hall that they owned on the site of the current Woolworth's building. After ten years, the site was cleared for development, and the school moved to a new site in Moss Street provided by the Earl of Seafield. Money for the building was raised locally and from Elgin friends abroad. It was completed by May 1837. The schoolmaster had no salary, and existed on whatever fees he could get from his pupils and on the produce of his large garden. The Trade School continued until School Boards came into existence in 1875. The site is now a row of shops on the east side of Moss Street.

The Art and Science School (1831-1914) evolved from the drawing school that was started by a group of students who wanted to further their knowledge of mechanical drawing. It first occupied a room in the Academy, but later moved to Newmill factory. In 1875 the school moved to Holy Trinity Church Hall, and then in 1882 to the supper room of the Town Hall in Moray Street. At last, in 1890, the drawing school moved into a building of its own: the Town Council had built one to commemorate the Jubilee of Queen Victoria. It was named The Victoria School of Art and Science, and it was opened by Queen Victoria's grand-daughter, the Princess Royal, in 1889. It is in Moray Street, opposite Moray College, which now has the use of it.

The East End School, designed by Archibald Simpson of Aberdeen, was built between 1830 and 1833 at the same time as Anderson's Institution. Its style is classical, similar to Anderson's Institution itself, and its lodge has an interesting twisted chimney. The Ragged School (1856-78), held in a house in Lady Lane at the foot of Ladyhill, provided elementary education to children whose parents were too poor to clothe them decently and quite unable to pay the fees asked for by other schools.

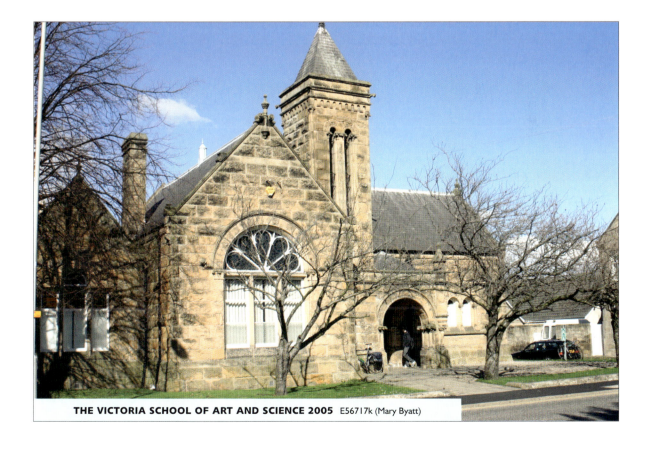

THE VICTORIA SCHOOL OF ART AND SCIENCE 2005 E56717k (Mary Byatt)

Weston House School (1856-74) arose out of a dispute between church and state over control of Elgin Academy. The established church disapproved of the appointment of a classics master, Mr Morrison, who belonged to the Free Church and who refused to sign the Confession of Faith and Formula of Worship. Mr Morrison resigned, and taking all his boarding pupils with him, set up a boarding school for the sons of gentlemen at the north end of Hay Street. It was very successful academically. In 1864 Alexander Graham Bell, who invented the telephone, became an assistant master in elocution and music at Weston House School. His father, also a professional elocutionist, had been appointed headmaster there. The school has been demolished, and a modern building used by the electrical retailer Comet is now on the site. A framed notice commemorating Bell's association with Elgin hangs next to the telephone sales stand inside the shop.

The Educational Institute (1874-79) took over when the Weston House School closed. The Station Hotel was bought to house it, and its purpose was the education of children of the 'highest class'. The Elgin High School (1881-83) was held in the Evangelists' Hall in South Street, and arose out of dissatisfaction with Elgin Academy. Although it only lasted short while, its existence made a statement that helped to force changes at the Elgin Academy and restore it to its former prestige.

THE ELGIN CLUB

In 1863, a group of eminent local gentlemen met regularly in a rented room in the Assembly Rooms building and installed a billiard table. They found their meetings so congenial and free from 'domestic obligations' that they proposed forming a club. By February 1864 they had drawn up a constitution and decided to engage a 'man' who would look after their needs. Their first employee was a lame soldier who had returned from service in India. He and his wife served the Elgin Club well for the first 23 years of its life, moving with it in 1869 to purpose-built premises in Commerce Street. This palazzo-style building is another of A & W Reid's masterpieces, and has a domed billiard room on the first floor.

THE MONOGRAM OF THE ELGIN CLUB 2005
ZZZ04321 (Mary Byatt)

This is carved above the Elgin Club's doorway in Commerce Street.

Presidents of the Elgin Club lasted longer than their servants. The first president was Hugh MacLean of Westfield, and by 1984 there had been just ten other presidents. In the same period of time the post of caretaker had been filled and vacated 21 times, some caretakers lasting less than a year.

For many years the club was used as a popular drinking house as well as for billiards and cards. By the mid 20th century the membership had dropped, and the place was threatened with closure. In 1970 a catering business was set up within the club, and women were admitted in an effort to attract more members. The Elgin Club continued until 2003, but in the end it had to close - the way of life in the 21st century is so very different to that of Victorian Elgin. Planning permission is currently being sought to turn the building into a casino.

THE ELGIN MUSEUM

The Elgin Museum was built for The Elgin & Morayshire Scientific Society and remains one of the only purpose-built museums in Scotland still owned and run by the society that built it - albeit under the changed name of The Moray Society. It is arguably the first purpose-built museum planned in Scotland, but it took five years for the plan to come to fruition. Montrose museum was finished in 1842, a year earlier, making The Elgin Museum (opened in 1843) the second to be completed.

The principal founder of the museum was the Rev Dr George Gordon, for 57 years minister of Birnie. 'In the world of science,

THE ELGIN MUSEUM c1850 EM00024 (The Elgin Museum)

he acquired and maintained till the day of his death a fame and a reputation unequalled in Scotland ... There was nothing in the earth, air or water that escaped the notice of Dr Gordon'. (Cosmo Innes, Sheriff). Other notable individuals amongst its 26 founder members were Patrick Duff, geologist, Isaac Forsyth, bookseller, and John Martin, who became the first curator of the museum.

By 1837 these founding gentlemen needed to find new premises to house their growing collection of local fossils, which they kept at that time in a room at the jail. A plot on which to build the museum was bought in 1838 for £60, and a plan by William Robertson approved. Fund-raising began, but William Robertson died in 1841, and a subsequent plan by Thomas Mackenzie was approved. The Italian style he chose was considered to be more suitable than the neo-classical style currently in use throughout Elgin. It was cheaper, and would provide better lighting. The museum was completed by 1843 at a cost of £975. The collections mushroomed, and Sheriff Cosmo Innes said in a lecture to the Elgin Scientific Society in 1860: 'Your museum provides a great amount of concentrated intelligence in antiquities and natural science'.

**THE REV DR GEORGE GORDON,
FOUNDER OF THE ELGIN MUSEUM c1890**
ZZZ04338 (The Elgin Museum)

From early on in its life, the museum was associated with important men of science such as Sir Roderick Murchison, T H Huxley, James Nicol, J W Judd, and Archibald Geikie. The archive of the Rev Dr George Gordon's correspondence contains letters from T H Huxley and Charles Darwin. Dr Gordon was a fine naturalist; he was also largely responsible for the museum's collection of fossil fish and reptiles, unique to the Elgin area. Many of the species are named after him

or after Elgin itself. The British Association of the time was aware of the importance of the sandstone formations that had been revealed in the quarries north of Elgin.

As the years passed, further space was required for the growing collection of fossils and objects donated to the museum from overseas. A rear gallery was added in 1896, funded by the Earl of Moray. The museum hall was added in 1929 on the east side, using a design by Thomas Mackenzie's son, A Marshall Mackenzie.

ATTITUDES TO CHANGE

Inevitably the numerous changes that Elgin underwent during the first half of the 19th century were not acceptable to all. Sheriff Cosmo Innes wrote: 'The town is much changed of late. St Giles Church, of venerable antiquity, has given way to a gay new edifice. The dwellings of the citizens have put on a modern trim look, which does not satisfy the eye so well as the sober grey walls of their fathers. Numerous hospitals, the fruits of mixed charity and vanity, surround the town with their gaudy white porticos, and contrast offensively with the mellow colouring and chaste proportions of the ancient structures. If the present taste continues, there will soon be nothing remaining of the reverend antique town, but the ruins of its magnificent cathedral.'

As is so often the case, it was the older generations who found the changes most difficult to accept. William Hay wrote a fourteen-verse poem for the Edinburgh Morayshire Society entitled 'When This Auld

The Elgin Poet, William Hay, 1794-1854

Like Gray and Anderson, William Hay was a 'lad o' pairts', born in White Horse Close, Elgin, to a poor mother. Various patrons noticed his lively nature. They sent him to Elgin Academy, where he proved an apt pupil. Later he lived in Edinburgh, and was appointed poet laureate to the Edinburgh Morayshire Society in 1828. He was the chief author of 'The Lintie of Moray', a collection of poems written to be sung at the end of the Edinburgh Morayshire Society's annual dinners. Here are two verses of his best-known ten-verse poem recounting the ostentatious entry of the town dignitaries into the Old Muckle Kirk:

But hark! The Bailies come,
　Wi' their officers before them;
Proud, could they now look up,
　Would the mithers be that bore them.
And having reach'd the door,
　Wi' their halberts form a sentry,
And while the Bailies pass,
　Stand booin' at the entry.

And now the Trades draw near,
　Wi' order and decorum,
And, proud as Bubly-Jocks,
　Their Deacons strut before 'em.
Their glory is so great,
　Oh! Let flesh and blood forgie them;
And as the folks gang in,
　So let us enter wi' them.

(Note: bubly-jocks are turkeys).

WILL HAY c1850 ZZZ04323 (The Elgin Museum)

Coat Was New'. In it he bemoans the passing of the old buildings:

> *'What a goodly town it was*
> *When this auld coat was new, Sir!*
> *Chorus: Elgin was a toon*
> *A toon to live an' dee in;*
> *But noo it is a hole,*
> *Which few would care to be in.'*

Despite the regret of the older generations, life for most people in Elgin was definitely getting easier. The amenities improved dramatically with the arrival of gas in 1830 and of running water in 1840. The Elgin Gas-light Company was formed in 1830, and the first gas works were built between Lossie Green and the Cooper Park. In 1931 they were moved to Pinefield, where they were enlarged. There are no gasworks in Elgin now.

Elgin's West End fountain was built in 1892 by the Elgin Amenity Association. It is a circular drinking trough topped by a wrought iron lamp, and was supposed to be a convenient watering point. It was removed in 1949 when the roundabout at Dr Gray's Hospital was built. The Elgin Fund has recently paid for it to be re-erected on the pavement beside the entrance to the hospital.

ELGIN'S BRIDGES

One of Elgin's most appealing features is the River Lossie, which encloses the city on three sides as it winds its way northwards. You are unaware of it unless you make a point of walking its course from the Haugh in the west and round Borough Briggs and Cooper Park to the cathedral in the east. The Lossie is known to have changed its course several times through the once wet, marshy area of Borough Briggs, and may at one time have run closer to the town near today's Town Hall. It is not surprising, then, that water laps its steps when the river floods today.

Starting upstream of Elgin at Palmerscross, there are thirteen river crossings, one rail bridge, nine road bridges and three footbridges. Many of the bridges are at the sites of old corn mills, and still bear the mills' names. The oldest existing stone bridge is Bow Brig (number 4 on the map, page 83, ZZZ04322), built between 1630 and 1635. At that time, all other river crossings were fords. For over 150 years, Bow Brig was the only stone bridge across the Lossie. It was remodelled in 1789 and survived the Muckle Spate of 1829 unscathed.

In 1801 and 1802 the Treasury commissioned surveys by Telford; he proposed a network of roads and bridges through northeast Scotland, resulting in the building of a turnpike road from the Spey to Nairn, which crossed the Lossie at Sheriffmill (3), where a two-arched bridge was constructed in 1803.

Brewery Bridge (11) was also built in 1803. It is a two-arched stone bridge, and gets its name from the now-demolished brewery beside the cathedral. It is now closed to vehicles and used only as a footbridge. Palmerscross Bridge (1) was built in 1814, a two-arched stone bridge replacing an old wooden bridge on stone piers that had lasted since 1755. Before 1755 it was a 'palmer's fiurd', used by pilgrims with palmer's staff and gown walking between Pluscarden Abbey and Elgin Cathedral. The next bridge to be built was the 1826 wooden bridge at Deanshaugh (10) near the cathedral. It was washed away three years later by the 1829 floods; then its replacement was washed away in 1882. A suspension bridge named the White Bridge on account of its white paint was opened in 1883. The current concrete bridge built was built in 1970. The Marywell Foot Bridge (6), a light iron bridge near the Haugh, was built around 1870, replacing a wooden bridge built in 1848.

Morriston Bridge (7), at Blackfriars Haugh, is a Bailey bridge serving the King George V memorial playing field. There was once a footbridge here over a ford. Bishopmill Old Bridge (9), the Red Bridge, was built in 1872. It is now closed to vehicles but open as a footbridge. Newmill Bridge (12) nearby was constructed in 1968/70 when Pansport Road was realigned to bypass Brewery Bridge. Connet Hill Bridge (2), a new two-arch bridge completed in 1956, was made necessary by the re-alignment of the A96 to the south of Sheriffmill. Bishopmill New Bridge (8) was

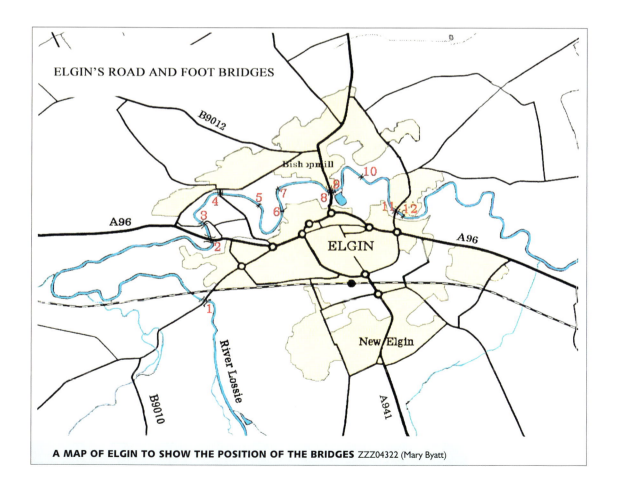

ELGIN'S ROAD AND FOOT BRIDGES

A MAP OF ELGIN TO SHOW THE POSITION OF THE BRIDGES ZZZ04322 (Mary Byatt)

SHERIFFMILL BRIDGE EM00026 (The Elgin Museum)

built in 1987/88 to cater for increased traffic on the Elgin to Lossiemouth road. The most recent bridge is Oldmills Foot Bridge (5), built in 1985 by No 2 Troop of 118 Field Squadron Royal Engineers.

TRANSPORT

Mail was carried on horseback three times a week between Elgin and Aberdeen until 1812, when a two-horse mail coach from Aberdeen to Inverness was established. In 1819 a four-horse coach, the Duke of Gordon, started up; it left Inverness daily at 6 am, reaching Elgin by midday and Aberdeen by 10 pm. The regular mail coach added two more horses in

order to compete. From 1826, two separate Star coaches were instituted, one from Elgin to Inverness, and the other from Aberdeen to Elgin. The coaches continued until they were superseded by the railways.

The locally financed Morayshire Railway opened a line from Lossiemouth harbour to Elgin in 1852 and completed a line from Elgin to Strathspey in 1863. The company merged with the Great North of Scotland Railway in 1880. The Great North of Scotland Railway started building a line from Aberdeen to Inverness in 1852, getting as far as Huntly by 1854 and Keith two years later. Inverness folk got tired of waiting, and set up their own railway company (The Inverness & Elgin Company) to build a line as far as Nairn and beyond. Needless to say, there ensued a great controversy between the two railway companies as to who owned the right to build a line on the land between Keith and Nairn. At one time, agreement was reached that the two companies should each build as far as the Spey and then share the cost of bridging it. The bill to

BOW BRIG 2005 E56718k (Mary Byatt)

get this proposal passed by Parliament failed; in the meantime, the Inverness & Elgin Company was dissolved and a new company formed called the Inverness & Aberdeen Junction Railway. With a subscription of £40,000 from the Great North of Scotland Railway and two of their directors on board, this new company built the railway right through to Keith. The line opened to rail traffic in 1858.

Queen Victoria, who frequently travelled by railway, was persuaded to stop at Elgin in 1872 on her way north to Dunrobin Castle. 'The Provost, Magistrates, and whole other office-bearers met in the Council Room ... and being there joined by His Grace the Duke of Richmond and the Earl of March, proceeded to the Highland Railway Station to await Her Majesty's arrival, where there was a dense crowd of the respectable classes

of the town and surrounding countryside assembled. All was in the greatest order, triumphal arches being erected, with banners and other emblems of loyalty. Her Majesty's special train arrived about 2 o'clock, with Earl Granville, Secretary of State in attendance. On reaching the landing platform, Her Majesty's state carriage was opened, and the Queen appeared at the door. She seemed in excellent spirits, and much pleased with the appearance of the large assemblage met to do her honour. The Loyal Address of Elgin Town Council was duly presented by the Provost and graciously received ... After remaining about a quarter of an hour, the Royal train departed for the north amidst the plaudits of the numerous spectators. It is believed that no sovereign had passed through Elgin since the time of the unfortunate Queen Mary in the year 1562'. (Youngs 'Annals of Elgin'.)

AWAITING THE ARRIVAL OF QUEEN VICTORIA AT ELGIN STATION 1872 EM00025 (The Elgin Museum)

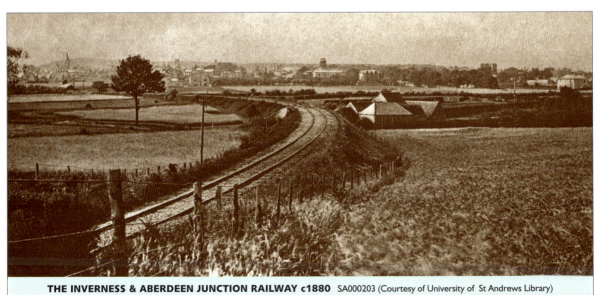

THE INVERNESS & ABERDEEN JUNCTION RAILWAY c1880 SA000203 (Courtesy of University of St Andrews Library)

Elgin has had a succession of railway stations. Queen Victoria's visit was photographed at an early station named the Highland Railway Station. The large and imposing Great North of Scotland Railway Station was built in 1898 to the east of the Rothes road, and was designed by P M Barnett. The railway station moved back to the west of the Rothes road in 1971, leaving the NSR station as a goods station only. With the coming of the railway, Commerce Street became the main route between the town centre and the station, and was widened accordingly.

ELGIN TOWN CENTRE 1884 EM00027 (The Elgin Museum)

This photograph shows the High Street, with relatively low buildings beyond St Giles.

INDUSTRY

Moray has long been known for its famous malt whiskies, and the duties imposed have always been an important source of revenue. Many illicit stills existed up in the hills at the start of the 19th century. In order to regularise the industry, the price of a licence for distilling was lowered in 1824 and the penalty for unlicensed distilling increased to £20. The legalised distilleries prospered, and malt whisky became one of Moray's prime exports. Many large distilleries were built in the glens of Moray. Elgin has two distilleries within its boundary, the Glen Moray Distillery and the Linkwood Distillery. Glen Moray Distillery (1897) was built on the site of the old West Brewery, several of the old buildings being incorporated into the new. A special water supply was laid on from the town's supply and electricity was supplied throughout. At that time there were twelve distilleries in the area, and more under construction.

Two businesses that started at the very beginning of the 19th century were to become major employers that brought wealth to the town. They were the Elgin Tan Works and Johnstons wool mill. The tan works was started in 1801 by Mr Alexander Culbard, a glover. It was sited on the east side of Lossie Wynd, and had tan pits and buildings for dressing skins. Alexander Culbard's son, James, joined the family business in 1839 and purchased land to the west of Lossie Wynd. Here he extended and improved the works, making it the largest in the north of Scotland. Trade was carried out both throughout Scotland and as far south as London. James Culbard used not only local skins but also imported hides from Denmark and Russia. He died in 1860 and was succeeded by his son William. With the introduction of steam engines and hydraulic presses, William Culbard now had a works that could dress and finish leather for the very best markets. He also traded in wool, and had a large drying loft that extended the length of his range of buildings. He employed 40 to 50 men and boys, and his business reached most of the principal towns in England and Scotland.

The second major business, Johnstons, started in 1800 when Alexander Johnston took on the meal and carding mill at Newmill. Initially he imported flax and wove linen, but this was phased out after the first ten years, and the weaving of woollen cloth took over. He was an entrepreneur, with fingers in many pies. He grew oats and ground them in the Newmill corn mill, as well as dabbling in the tobacco and snuff trade. He even had shares in coasters and sold herrings.

CELEBRATIONS IN ELGIN TOWN CENTRE ON 27 JULY 1889 EM00028 (The Elgin Museum)

The celebrations marked the marriage of Queen Victoria's grand-daughter, Louise, Princess Royal, to Alexander Duff, Duke of Fife.

It was this entrepreneurial gift that enabled him to survive the vicissitudes of the cloth trade and to build up a company with a national reputation, trading with London, Glasgow and Edinburgh. He was joined by his son James in 1838, and retired in 1846. James Johnston was an experimenter. He pioneered the weaving of vicuna and cashmere, first importing the raw materials in 1851. The company became known for its 'estate tweeds', and was the first to weave lovat tweed for Lord Lovat - lovat is now an adjective in common use in the woollen trade. The output of the mill was diverse, from simple blues and serges for sailors and soldiers to sophisticated angora and cashmere. The huge plaids (54 inches by 5 yards) were popular with early travellers, but were superseded by rugs when coach travel came in. James Johnston exhibited in the Great Exhibition of 1851 in London and in the Paris exhibition in 1855. His son Charles joined the business a dozen years later. Trade collapsed in 1873, but soon recovered when sales to the USA started in 1882. America became the main export market, with Brooks Bros of New York as well-known customers. The company by then employed nearly 200 people, and ran an iron forge and engineering works as well. Initially this was established to repair the plant of the woollen mill, but later it took on custom from outside and supplied steam engines, reaping machines and 'other miscellaneous articles of a regular engineering works'.

THE MORAYSHIRE UNION POORHOUSE

Up until the Reformation, the church took care of the poor and dispossessed. Thereafter they were less well catered for, and begging was commonplace. The Poor Law tried to put a stop to begging, and Elgin's Poorhouse was built in 1865, situated at the north end of the village of Bishopmill. Although well cared for, the poor made every effort not to be sent there, as they disliked being confined. The women had to wear purple uniform dresses, one of which is on display in the Elgin Museum. Elgin's famous poet, William Hay Leith Tester ('La Teste'), ended his days in the Poorhouse. He christened it 'Peter's Palace' after the governor, Peter Grant:

'Peter get your palace ready,
Tak' us a' tae Bishopmill
We're hungry, haggard, naked, needy,
Be thou our good St Peter still.'

This is the last verse of a fourteen-verse poem, much of which describes the plight of the poor. Craigmoray, the Morayshire Union Poorhouse, was demolished in the early 1970s.

CHAPTER FOUR

Of War and Peace – 1900 to 1999

HIGH STREET c1910 EM00045 (The Elgin Museum)

ELGIN was now a prosperous town with a re-established coat of arms (see Topic Box, page 92). The Lord Provost's house boasted a pair of special wrought iron street lamps with the Elgin coats of arms on their glass. When the post of Lord Provost was abolished in 1975, the lamps stayed in the front garden of the house of the last provost. This house is beside the Dr Gray's roundabout, and the brightly coloured Elgin coats of arms on the glass facets of the lamps can easily be seen from the road.

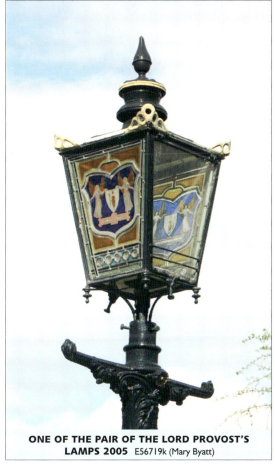

ONE OF THE PAIR OF THE LORD PROVOST'S LAMPS 2005 E56719k (Mary Byatt)

The Arms of the Royal Burgh of Elgin

The arms of Elgin were granted in 1678, but were 'lost' for two centuries until they were re-discovered through the perseverance of some persistent Victorian gentlemen. They were recorded with the Lord Lyon in 1888. The arms feature St Giles carrying a pastoral staff in his right hand and a book in his left hand. He stands on a compartment of bricks, signifying a burgh, and is supported by two gold-winged angels flying upwards. In heraldic terms the arms are described thus: 'Argent Sanctus Aegidius habited in his robes and mitred holding in his dexter hand a Pastoral Staff and in his left hand a clasped Book all proper: supported by two Angels proper winged Or volant upwards and the Motto, 'Sic itur ad astra' upon ane compartment suitabill to a Burgh Royal and for their colours Red and White'.

THE ARMS OF THE ROYAL BURGH OF ELGIN 1888
ZZZ04324 (Messrs Thorburn)

The relatively peaceful years of the early 20th century saw more substantial buildings going up in Elgin. A large draper's store, Ramsay's, was built in 1903 on the north side of the High Street, at Nos 123-133. Some 90 years later the area behind this building was converted to a shopping centre - the St Giles Centre - and the Edwardian façade with its high roofline was kept intact.

Grant Lodge (built in 1750), originally the town house of the Seafield family, was gifted to the town of Elgin in 1903 by the then owner, Sir George Cooper. The 40 acres of land that went with it were laid out as a park by A Marshall Mackenzie, and renamed

A L RAMSAY & SON, DRAPERS c1905
EM00029 (The Elgin Museum)

the Cooper Park. The Cooper Park has gone from strength to strength and now has a nine-hole pitch and putt course, putting greens, a public bowling green, a boating pond, tennis courts and an aviary. The Drill Hall was built at one end of the Cooper Park three years after the opening ceremony. It was built for the 6th Volunteer Battalion of the Seaforth Highlanders, and it housed the town's first gym.

At the time of the opening of the park the public library was transferred to Grant Lodge from a side room of the Town Hall. By 1992 the library had outgrown the space available in Grant Lodge and it was moved to the Drill Hall, which was by then no longer used by the army. In 1997 the library moved again, this time to a purpose-built building next door to the Drill Hall. Meanwhile, Grant Lodge was used to house the valuable local history reference library. Sad to say, a fire in 2003 necessitated the removal of all the valuable books and documents it contained, and the building was boarded up.

St Columba's Church, Moss Street, was built in 1906 to cope with the ever-growing congregation of St Giles's in the High Street. Its designer, Peter MacGregor Chalmers, gave it soaring Romanesque arches and capitals decorated with Celtic carvings. The 1694 pulpit from the Muckle Kirk was brought back from Pluscarden and installed in the new church.

THE OPENING OF THE COOPER PARK AT GRANT LODGE 1903 EM00030 (The Elgin Museum)

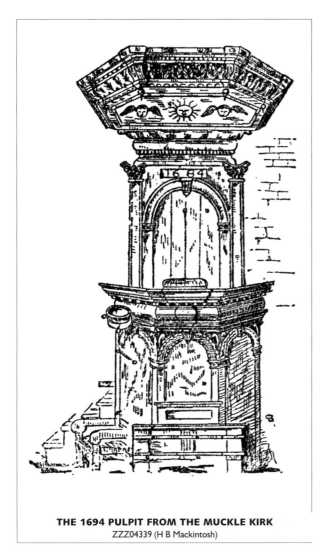

THE 1694 PULPIT FROM THE MUCKLE KIRK
ZZZ04339 (H B Mackintosh)

This pulpit is now in St Columba's Church, Moss Street.

THE FIRST WORLD WAR

The Morayshire Seaforth Highlanders were mobilised in the first week of August 1914. The task of notifying 900 men that their services were required was no light one. Motorcars, motorcycles and cycles were pressed into service to distribute the post office's bundles of notices. Men marched in from the surrounding countryside and were quartered on the drill hall in the Cooper Park before being taken by train to Invergordon. The citizens of Elgin turned out in large numbers to give the Seaforths a rousing send-off from the station.

TROOPS DEPARTING FROM ELGIN STATION 1914
EM00031 (The Elgin Museum)

As more and more men were called up, hardly a day passed in Elgin without the sound of marching feet, the beat of the drum and the thrill of the bagpipes. Sad to say, it was not long before some of the men were wounded and sent home for treatment and convalescence. A house known as Oakbank was made available to the Red Cross early in the war, and of course Dr Gray's Hospital was used too. Gordon Castle at Fochabers became the principal convalescent home. During the First World War, Elgin experienced one of its worst floods. The photographs opposite show a troop train leaving Elgin station in 1915 and workers in Johnstons Mill surveying damaged goods.

A TROOP TRAIN LEAVING ELGIN IN THE FLOODS 1915 EM00032 (The Elgin Museum)

FLOOD-DAMAGED GOODS IN JOHNSTONS WOOL MILL 1915 EM00033 (The Elgin Museum)

In 1918, Sir Archibald Williamson, MP for Moray and Nairn, donated two war veterans' cottages and a Memorial Garden 'in commemoration of the termination of the Great War'. They were built at the foot of Ladyhill in 1919. Each cottage has a sheltered arcade incorporating old carved stones.

The deaths of 461 men of Elgin in the Great War are recorded on the war memorial designed by Percy Portsmouth on the Plainstones. It was unveiled in December 1921 before a crowd of about 5,000 people. It is now a joint memorial for the First World War and the Second World War.

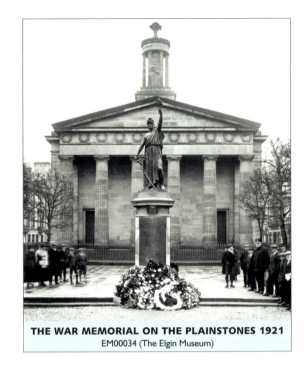

THE WAR MEMORIAL ON THE PLAINSTONES 1921
EM00034 (The Elgin Museum)

THE MEMORIAL GARDENS AT THE FOOT OF LADYHILL 2005 E56720k (Mary Byatt)

Did you know?

The figure on top of the war memorial on the Plainstones in Elgin is a bronze statue of Victory.

TRANSPORT

The Elgin & District Bus Company was inaugurated in 1919. It ran one bus continuously between the Plainstones in Elgin and Stotfield in Lossiemouth; it was particularly popular on a Friday, the day of the Elgin farmers' market. The return fare was just sixpence, and the railways had to reduce their fares in order to compete. A second route was added in 1920, running between Elgin and Burghead via Duffus and Hopeman. Then a service to Keith was added.

The first buses were 32-seater Albion buses with paraffin headlamps and chain-driven wheels with solid tyres. They cost over £1,000, and Elgin folk often had to put up with second-hand vehicles as a result. The driver's weekly wage was £2 10s, and the conductor was paid just 12s 6d per week. Both of them routinely worked up to 20 hours a day, as there was no limit to the service provided.

THE BURGHEAD BUS 1920 EM00035 (The Elgin Museum)

THE CUMMING STREET BUS STATION c1960 ZZZ04644
(Reproduced by kind permission of the Editor, The Northern Scot)

by a crowd of 10,000 people. In 1991, Elgin Rotary devised the city marathon, or 'Marafun', a fund-raising relay race of marathon length held within the city - the idea of holding a Marafun has been adopted by other Rotary clubs in Scotland. The Rotary Club of Elgin is extremely active. It has a membership of 74, and has had many accolades from Rotary International for its service to the community, both locally and internationally.

RAMSAY MACDONALD

Moray's James Ramsay Macdonald, brought up in Lossiemouth, became the first Labour prime minister in 1924. He started his second term of office in 1928, and was granted freedom of the City of Elgin in August 1929. The Elgin Museum has a fine bronze sculpture of him by Jacob Epstein.

The Cumming Street bus station was built in 1953, and was in operation until the relief road was built through it in 1978. Buses now operate from a new station at the back of the St Giles Centre.

THE ROTARY CLUB OF ELGIN

E S Harrison of Johnstons Mill founded the Rotary Club of Elgin in 1927 and was its first president until 1928. The Rotary has held several galas in the Cooper Park over the years; the most memorable was the 'Taste of Moray' Gala of 1983. It was attended by HRH Princess Margaret, who was welcomed

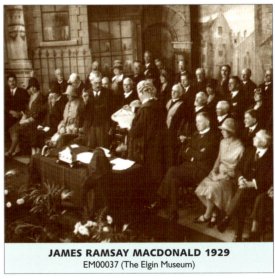

JAMES RAMSAY MACDONALD 1929
EM00037 (The Elgin Museum)

This photograph shows Ramsay Macdonald being granted the Freedom of the City of Elgin.

THE SECOND WORLD WAR

By 1938 war was anticipated, and a purpose-built camp for training volunteers and conscripts was put up at Pinefield on the east of Elgin. During the war, the camp was used to house the Royal Engineers and the cadets under training. Elgin's battalion, the 6th Seaforth Highlanders, was mobilised on 30 August 1939, four days before war was declared. The battalion's headquarters was the drill hall in the Cooper Park.

During the early part of the war, Elgin took in evacuees from Edinburgh; two trainloads arrived on 2 September 1939. When it was realised that Edinburgh was not a target for German bombs, they drifted home again, and were probably all home by Christmas 1939.

In response to an apparent shortage of aluminium for manufacture of aircraft, Elgin households collected all their spare pots and pans, and a huge pile grew up somewhere near the drill hall. No doubt the effect on the aluminium supply was minimal, but everyone felt they were doing their bit for the war effort. Iron was collected too, and this had a lasting effect upon Elgin. All through the town there are low walls with the sawn-off stumps of Victorian iron railings. It is a shame that the iron collected was probably never used.

Civilian life was affected from the outset of the war by the introduction of total blackout after dark from 1 September 1939. Streetlights were turned off, and houses were not allowed to show the slightest chink of light. A torch could only be used if its beam measured no more than one inch in diameter, so movement after dark was very difficult. Car headlamps were hooded and sidelights dimmed. As a result there were frequent accidents until shortage of petrol limited the use of cars. Gas masks were issued to everyone at the start of the war; small children were given brightly coloured red and blue ones, while older children had to make do with the standard issue. Food rationing started in January 1940 and was not totally abolished until the 1950s. Ration books were issued from South Villa in Moss Street, once the town house of the Grants of Elchies.

No enemy bombs fell on Elgin, but after the German occupation of Norway in 1940, it was feared that the Germans might well invade through the beaches of northeast Scotland. The threat of invasion was countered by the formation of the Moray Local Defence Volunteers, manned largely by farm workers. The LDF later became the Home Guard, with Colonel J O Hopkinson MC DSO as its first commander. He had served in Somalia and then in the First World War. He was succeeded in 1942 by Lieutenant Colonel John Petrie of Newton, a man of less military experience, but highly successful as a leader. By 1942 the Home Guard was very different from the once eager but untrained LDV. It trained men for the regular army, and manned local anti-aircraft equipment, coastal batteries, and local gun emplacements. Petrie remained the commanding officer until the stand down on Wednesday

1 November 1944. He is seen in ZZZ04325 (centre right, front row) with the members of the 1st Moray Battalion Home Guard and with the battalion's pipe band.

Moray's flat land and fog-free climate made it suitable for airfields. There were airfields all around Moray, and the bombing of the 'Tirpitz', sister ship to the 'Bismarck', took place out of Lossiemouth airfield.

All beaches from Macduff to Nairn were heavily mined, and lines of anti-tank concrete blocks were built along them, with pillboxes at intervals. During the winter of 1943-44, Moray beaches were used to train for the D-day landings: an area of land north of a line from Dyke to Alves as far as the coast was evacuated from August 1943 for six months, and people were given just six weeks' notice to leave their houses.

THE ATC MARCHING THROUGH ELGIN 1944
ZZZ04326 (Reproduced by kind permission of the Editor, The Northern Scot)

The main building behind them is the Gordon Arms Hotel, now Burtons.

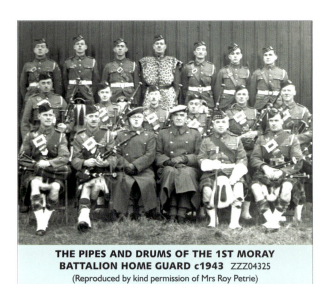

THE PIPES AND DRUMS OF THE 1ST MORAY BATTALION HOME GUARD c1943 ZZZ04325
(Reproduced by kind permission of Mrs Roy Petrie)

The Commanding Officer, Lieutenant Colonel John Petrie, is seated centre right. Captain & Adjutant A A Campbell is to the centre left.

After the war, the Pinefield Camp became Pinefield Industrial Estate. Many of the original prefabricated wooden huts are still in usc, some having been clad in brick in the 1950s.

FARMING

Before the Second World War, farm work was largely unmechanised except for threshing. Most farms were using Clydesdale horses, and very few had tractors.

Alexander Mitchell Ferrier, a War Hero

Alexander Ferrier, an Elgin loon (boy), joined the navy in 1936, trained as a signalman and then served on the Polish destroyer 'Grom', which was bombed and sunk in 1940. He was awarded the Polish Cross of Valour for his bravery. Later he was at Dunkirk and Le Havre, where he received severe shrapnel wounds. In 1942 Leading Signalman Ferrier was asked to join another officer on special secret duties. He was trained to operate a two-man chariot (a midget submarine with two seats); on 3 January 1943 he rode pillion into Palermo harbour, where the newly built Italian cruiser 'Ulpio Traiano' was being fitted out for service. He and his leader, Lieutenant Richard Greenland, dived under the ship, fixed limpet charges and set fuses. The ship was successfully blown up and sunk, but the pair were caught and imprisoned. At first they were held in Italy, and then later in Germany. Alexander Ferrier was awarded the Conspicuous Gallantry Medal, and Richard Greenland was awarded the DSO. After the war, a new housing development in Bishopmill was named Ferrier Terrace.

PLOUGHING WITH HORSES c1930   EM00038 (The Elgin Museum)

Farm workers were poorly paid, and were employed on a seasonal basis. They would attend twice yearly 'feeing marts', where they milled about, many of them looking for jobs, and some hoping to be offered better employment than they already had. Faced with the need to grow more food in the war, the government funded the changeover from horses to tractors. German and Italian POWs and girls of the Women's Land Army helped on farms, and at the end of the war farmers were considerably better off than they had been in the 1930s. Many of the Italian POWs settled in Moray and were absorbed into the community.

JOHNSTONS OF ELGIN

At the beginning of the 20th century, Johnstons Mill was still powered by a single, central steam engine, assisted by a water wheel. If anything went wrong, the whole plant stopped working. In 1908 four separate gas-driven engines were installed, each supplying a different department, so total stoppages were no longer possible.

Charles Johnston, the founder's grandson, lost his enthusiasm for the business when his son was killed in the First World War. He sold his interest in the firm to an employee, Edward Harrison, who was keenly interested in the design and production of cloth. On a visit to America, Harrison saw that there would be demand for a lighter, looser cloth than tweed. His idea resulted in a lucrative scarf trade that kept Johnstons going through the dark days of the Depression. During the Second World War all woollen companies had to make quotas of khaki cloth for the army, and of utility cloth for sale on coupons to the general public. Any time left over was devoted to the making of scarves, which were sent to America by parcel post throughout the war. Harrison Terrace in Bishopmill was built in 1949; it is named after Edward Harrison, who was by then Lord Provost. His son, Ned, became chairman of Johnstons in 1966, and his nephew, John, succeeded him in 1978. Johnstons won the Queen's Award for Export in 1978 and again in 1994. It has a worldwide reputation for the excellence of its products,

AN EARLY THRESHING MACHINE AT THE BEGINNING OF THE 20TH CENTURY EM00039 (The Elgin Museum)

and its mill shop, the Cashmere Centre, attracts tourists from all over the world.

GORDON & MACPHAIL

One of Elgin's most successful businesses is Gordon & MacPhail, a grocer's and malt whisky specialist. Started in 1895 by James Gordon, a much-travelled wholesaler, and John Alexander MacPhail, it has grown into a company employing more than 100 people. The whisky boom had started in 1895, but overproduction caused a collapse of the industry in 1899, and many distilleries had to close. Gordon & MacPhail had had the foresight to fill casks that gave them a stock when the whisky supply fell. As well as a steady commitment to the grocery side of the business, they continued to supply customers with malt whisky straight from the cask. John MacPhail retired in 1915 and was replaced by John Urquhart. Just two weeks later James Gordon was killed in a car crash; John Urquhart became senior partner, with Mrs Gordon as a partner working alongside him. After the end of the Second World War the firm started exporting Highland malt whisky. Some of this whisky had been kept to mature longer than usual. Large numbers of barrels were filled in the late 1930s, and although some was released during the Second World War for shipment to America to earn dollars, the company still had a healthy stock after the war. By 1960, huge bonded warehouses had been erected on Borough Briggs Road. The list of countries supplied with malt whisky has grown and grown, with at least half of the

ONE OF JOHNSTONS MONSTER BOILERS ARRIVING
1908 ZZZ04645 (The Northern Scot)

JOHNSTONS CASHMERE CENTRE 2005 ZZZ04327 (Mary Byatt)

GORDON & MACPHAIL'S SOUTH STREET GROCER'S
SHOP 2005 E56721k (Mary Byatt)

exported whisky having been matured in expensive sherry casks.

The company's long-term wish to own a distillery and so produce its very own malt whisky was met with the purchase of Benromach Distillery in Forres. It had been mothballed for some years, and was re-opened in the late 20th century when it was purchased by Gordon & MacPhail. John Urquhart's youngest son George joined the firm in 1933, and his children all work for Gordon & MacPhail to this day. The grocer's is still in its original premises in South Street, and the whisky business is run from George House in front of the warehouses on Borough Briggs Road.

By 1961 Elgin's population had increased to 12,000, and its industries ranged from woollen mills to the manufacture of cod liver oil, fishing nets and lemonade.

LEISURE

Elgin once had two cinemas. The Picture House was built in South Street at the end of Fife Arms Close in 1926. The first talking picture to be seen in the north of Scotland was shown here. It is now a bingo hall. However, the Playhouse Cinema, built in 1932, continues to show the latest films.

Austin's tearooms in South Street no longer exist, but are fondly remembered by Elgin's older citizens as a genteel premises where you could partake of morning coffee or afternoon tea. The fine Art Deco interior of the first floor tearooms has been preserved. On the ground

floor was a baker's shop, which was said to be the best baker north of Perth, especially for 'fancies'. Mr Austin was an award-winning cake decorator.

FIFE ARMS CLOSE c1925 EM00041 (The Elgin Museum)

Here we see the site where the Picture House was to be built.

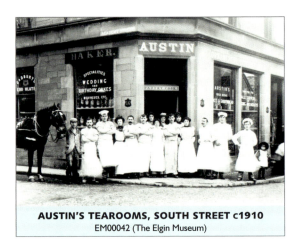

AUSTIN'S TEAROOMS, SOUTH STREET c1910
EM00042 (The Elgin Museum)

> ## Did you know?
>
> *Elgin's Playhouse Cinema was designed in 1932 by Alister Macdonald, son of James Ramsay Macdonald, the first Labour Prime Minister.*

Lossie Green was Elgin's main playground until the opening of the Cooper Park, and it is still used today by travelling circuses and fairs.

There have always been many opportunities for outdoor pursuits in and around Elgin.

THE SHOWIES ON LOSSIE GREEN c1910 ZZZ04646
(Reproduced by kind permission of the Editor, The Northern Scot)

One is Scotland's ancient game of golf. The earliest reference to golf in Elgin is in the Records of the Kirk Session in 1596, when a goldsmith named William Hay was *'accusit for playing at the boulis and golff upoun Sundaye in the tym of the sermon'*. Sunday golf was still an issue in 1604, when it was ordained from the pulpit that it be publicly banned. The first golf links were to the north of Elgin in a sandy, hillocky space, dotted with whins. Around 1760 it was realised that the land was potential farmland, and the golf links became Linksfield Farm. After that there was no golf in the area until the Moray Golf Club built its fine golf links at Lossiemouth in 1889. The Elgin Golf Club was established in 1906, and a golf course was laid out on the south side of New Elgin. Membership of Elgin Golf Club started at over 200, with a fee of just 10s 6d. By 1932, membership had reached 711, and a decision was taken to limit membership to 600 in the future.

Although there were once many other outdoor games carried out in Elgin, football has remained the most popular. The game was first mentioned in the 17th century, when it was little more than the chasing of an inflated pig's bladder around the Chanonry. It was disapproved of by the severe Calvinistic authorities of the time. Records of the Kirk Session of 1630 state that *'George Purse, James McWatty, Alexander Furnester for their playing at the futeball on the Sabbath nicht at even throw the calsey at ordeant ilk ane of them to pay 6s 8d'*. By 1888 there were several football clubs within Elgin. Football was played on the Grant Lodge lawn (by invitation), and at Kingsmills, Pansport, Moycroft and Market Green. From 1890 there was a District Cup, and in 1893 Elgin City FC and the Highland League were founded. The Elgin City football pitch was on Borough Briggs from1921. The 1930s were successful years for 'The City', with the Highland Flag being won for the first time in 1932 and again in 1935. But the 1960s were undoubtedly 'The City's' finest years, with the club coming first in the Highland League eight times. Elgin City joined the Scottish Football League in 2001. It is the most northerly national league club in Britain.

Elgin's most famous footballer was R C Hamilton, born in 1877, son of an Elgin net maker. He scored Elgin City's first goal on their Highland League debut against Inverness Citadel in 1895. After attending Glasgow University, R C Hamilton signed up as a professional with Rangers and was their leading goal scorer for nine seasons. R C Hamilton played for Scotland eleven times, scoring fifteen goals for his country. He played for various other clubs before retiring.

ELGIN CITY FOOTBALL TEAM 1895 ZZZ04328
(Reproduced by kind permission of the Editor, The Northern Scot)

R C Hamilton is seated in the centre front.

He returned home to Elgin, where he took part in two Scottish Qualifying Cup matches in 1913. He was elected to the town council in 1914, but was immediately sent to France to serve with the Cameron Highlanders. On his return he rejoined the town council and served on it until 1937, rising to position of Lord Provost in 1931. He ran the family net manufacturing business from 1913 until 1947, and died in 1948.

The Moray Leisure Centre was built in 1993 on the west side of Borough Briggs, and has enormously increased the opportunity for indoor exercise available to the people of Moray. It has a swimming pool, an ice rink, several gyms for fitness training, and is a popular and much-used facility.

NEW BUILDINGS

Elgin's town hall is a 1960s building situated beside Lossie Green. It was designed by Sir Basil Spence, and was built to replace A Marshall Mackenzie's imposing and ostentatious town hall, which was destroyed by fire in 1939.

The post office moved from Commerce Street in 1962 to a purpose-built place with a large sorting office at the west end of the High Street. It has since moved twice more, first to the Tesco building in Batchen Lane, and then to Batchen Street itself. The 1962 post office building is still used as a sorting office.

The Great North of Scotland Railway Station was abandoned in 1970 as a passenger station, and the majestic building of 1898 was replaced by a much smaller, flat-roofed building to the west, on the site of the old Highland Railway station. Twenty years later it was redesigned and smartened up, and Elgin once more had a reasonable station.

The Clydesdale Bank and Clydesdale Store on the north side of the High Street replaced the old Assembly Rooms and the 1857 North of Scotland Bank next door. Both buildings were complete by 1970, and add blank faces to an otherwise interesting and harmonious High Street (see photo in Chapter 3, page 69). At the same time Fine Fare, one of Elgin's first supermarkets, was built on the south side of the High Street, and introduced a faceless modern building to that side too. The building is now Boots the Chemists.

Dr Gray's Hospital, which had already had a wing added in 1939, was enormously expanded in the early 1990s at a cost of £22,000,000. The new building is of an interesting modern design, and, being at

THE TOWN HALL c1890 EM00044 (The Elgin Museum)

THE TOWN HALL ON FIRE 1939 ZZZ04329
(Reproduced by kind permission of the Editor, The Northern Scot)

the back, it has not altered the magnificent view of the original domed building from the east.

Murdoch's Wynd housing estate at the foot of Ladyhill was built in the early 1980s at a cost of £800,000. The 22-house estate was officially opened in 1985, and the development was given the top Saltire Society Award. It is a cleverly designed and most sympathetic development. Further housing estates have been built all around

Elgin, mostly to the north of Bishopmill and south of New Elgin, but also to the east at Pinefield and Linkwood. The population is now approaching 20,000.

RESTORATION

The cathedral is under the care of Historic Scotland, whose stone works next door have been used to dress stone to replace the tracery in the chapter house windows and elsewhere. The stonework of the east gable of the cathedral and its twin towers has also been repaired. The famous west towers of the cathedral have been roofed over, and access for the public has been provided. It is now possible to climb to the top of the most northerly of the twin towers and see fine views of Moray.

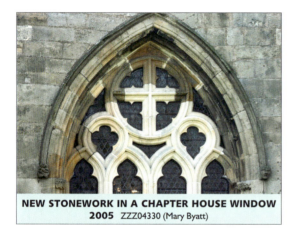

NEW STONEWORK IN A CHAPTER HOUSE WINDOW 2005 ZZZ04330 (Mary Byatt)

Each window of the octagonal chapter house has different tracery.

In 1964, the late E S Harrison of James Johnston & Company of Elgin founded the Elgin Fund. He was very interested in Elgin's past, and his aim was to contribute to the restoration of historic Elgin. The fund's first project was the restoration of the 18th-century Masonic Close buildings at the east end of the High Street, opposite the end of Glover Street. Since then the Elgin Fund has financed the restoration of the buildings at 30/32 High Street (next to the Moray council offices), the arcaded buildings at 44/46 High Street, and 225 High Street at the west end. It has also undertaken numerous paving projects within closes and the reconstruction of the Plainstones in front of St Giles's Church.

THE QUEEN WITH THE MINISTER OF ST GILES AND THE LORD PROVOST ZZZ04331
(Reproduced by kind permission of the Editor, The Northern Scot)

ROYAL VISITORS

Members of the royal family visited Elgin many times in the 20th century. Queen Elizabeth II paid an official visit in 1967 when Prince Charles was at Gordonstoun School nearby.

Prince Philip presented the colours to the 2nd battalion of the 51st Highland Volunteers in the Cooper Park on 26 June 1986, when Prince Edward was at Gordonstoun. The Princess Royal has also paid frequent visits to Elgin, where there is a flourishing branch of her Trust for Carers. On her last visit she was made an honorary member of the Elgin Rotary Club.

CHANGES IN THE TOWN PLAN

In the mid 20th century, Elgin's medieval town plan was still very evident and could have been preserved, but the demands of modern living won over: between 1979 and 1981 Elgin's controversial inner ring road was constructed. Whilst there is no doubt that it relieved the town centre of its hideous traffic problem, it cut the town off from its cathedral, severed the planned vista of North Street, ruined many old closes, and chopped off part of the Cooper Park into the bargain. A proper Elgin bypass has long been discussed, but it is still not built.

The centre of Elgin was pedestrianised in 1995 and was much improved as a result. Granite sets were imported from Portugal and laid in perfect fan shapes by Italian workmen. Fourteen maple trees were planted around St Giles's Kirk, and when holes were dug for them human bones from the old graveyard were found. On the Plainstones, a square plinth with

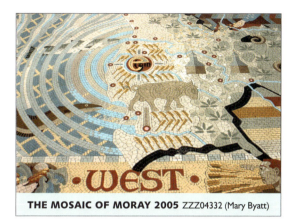

THE MOSAIC OF MORAY 2005 ZZZ04332 (Mary Byatt)

illustrated bronze plaques describes four aspects of Elgin's history, and a fine mosaic depicts aspects of life in Moray. Both are well worth studying.

The Biblical Garden

The biblical garden is adjacent to the cathedral. Walled on all sides, it is a wonderful haven of peace. It was opened in 1996 and was the first of its kind in Scotland. A huge Celtic cross of paving stones forms the basic structure of the garden. Paths around it divide the borders into areas that represent various habitats found in the Holy Land. The garden is said to contain 110 species of plants mentioned in the Bible, many of them donated by school groups in Moray. Life-size statues illustrate bible stories. The project was the collective brainchild of former staff of Moray District Council, and was funded by public subscription and donations from local businesses. The work was carried out by trainees from Moray Training as part of the council's rural skills initiative. Nowadays the garden is used by the horticultural department of Moray College as a teaching aid, and the flowerbeds are looked after by the students. The plaque at the entrance gives the following apt quotation:

'The kiss of the sun for pardon
The song of the birds for mirth
One is nearer God's heart in a garden
Than anywhere else on earth.'

(God's Garden, by Dorothy Gurney)

THE BIBLICAL GARDEN 2005 E56722k (Mary Byatt)

THE PAGEANT MARKING THE RE-OPENING OF THE ELGIN MUSEUM 2003 E56723k (Mary Byatt)

CHAPTER FIVE

The New Millennium –
2000 Onwards

ELGIN ENTERED the 21st century on a high note. Grampian Regional Council had been abolished in 1996 and control of the area had passed from Aberdeen back to Elgin, making it once more truly the capital of the area. A tastefully designed extension of the Moray council buildings was added to house extra offices.

Major refurbishment of the fabric of the Elgin Museum was completed in 2000, paid for largely by a grant from the Heritage Lottery Fund. The eroded and cracked stonework was refaced by Moray Stonecutters of Birnie, who had recently provided dressed sandstone for another museum, the prestigious National Museums of Scotland in Edinburgh. In 2002 a second, much larger, grant from the Heritage Lottery Fund enabled the Elgin Museum to refurbish its main gallery. Designers from Edinburgh and Glasgow were employed to bring the museum into the 21st century, and it closed for part of a season whilst major reorganisation was carried out inside. The museum was re-opened in August 2003 by Professor Tom Devine of Aberdeen University.

The Museum's New Exhibitions

The history of the fascinating little Elgin Museum is recorded in Chapter 3. It now houses two excellent displays, one in the north hall entitled 'The Making of Moray' and one in the main gallery, named 'People & Place'. The first of these was constructed in the 1980s, and won the Museum of the Year award in the early 1990s. It incorporates a display of the internationally renowned fossil fish and reptiles from the Elgin locality and some exceptional Pictish carved stones. The main gallery's 'People & Place' was designed after the millennium, and illustrates the history of Moray from AD 1000 to AD 2000. The aim of the designers was to make better use of the space available by constructing modern cases in the Victorian alcoves. As a result, it is now possible to display safely much more of the large collection of artefacts given over the years by Elgin people. Lack of space upstairs has prevented the installation of a lift, but people with disabilities can view the upstairs exhibits via a virtual tour on downstairs computer terminals. The museum is working on a database that will give relevant facts about all the people and places named in the exhibition.

THE NEW FACE OF THE MUSEUM 2005
E56724k (Mary Byatt)

INDUSTRY

A major new employer recently extended their business into Elgin; Walkers of Aberlour. A large shortbread factory was built on the south side of Elgin and opened by HRH Prince Charles, Duke of Rothesay, in 2001. Amongst its products are the new organic chocolate orange biscuits that Walkers produce for Duchy Originals Ltd. Walkers have been producing successive varieties of Duchy Original biscuits since 1992. They distribute their products to more than 60 overseas markets, and they won the Food Exporter of the Year award in 1996, 1999 and 2004. They were awarded the Highland Business of the Year award in 1986 and again in 2003, during which time their turnover had increased fourfold and their exports had increased eightfold. Walkers remains a family firm, and is now run by the grandchildren of the founder.

Another major local employer is the national building firm, Robertson Group, which has its main office in Elgin. The renowned family firm Baxters of Speyside also employs residents of Elgin, but has no base in the town.

Local firms have done much to help research and conserve Elgin's past by supporting its museum. There is strong

THE MEDIEVAL WELL 2004 ZZZ04333 (The Elgin Museum)

This was discovered recently on the Marks & Spencer site.

interest in any new archaeological work. Recently a building site at Lesmurdie, on the north side of Elgin, revealed unexpected evidence of Bronze Age activity preserved by deep topsoil. A ring ditch of unusually small size was excavated, and ash from cremations was found in it. The archaeologists also found several inverted collared urns that had been used for cremation burials. The area has since been covered with new housing.

A previously unknown medieval well, complete with its wooden fittings, was found towards the west end of the High Street when the foundations for the new Marks & Spencer were being dug in 2004.

Perhaps the greatest archaeological thrill of all has come from the discovery of two hoards of Roman coins in a field at Birnie, to the south of Elgin. Although evidence of Roman marching camps has been found, it is not thought that the Romans settled in Moray. The two pots of buried treasure may have been bribes to keep the local tribes quiet. Excavation of the site is ongoing under the direction of Fraser Hunter of the National Museums of Scotland, Edinburgh. The settlement at Birnie lasted from the Iron Age through to medieval times, and the coins date from the 2nd and 3rd centuries AD. The hoards were taken to Edinburgh for investigation and conservation. The first of the two is likely to be on display in the Elgin Museum by the end of 2005.

Restoration of historic Elgin goes on. The gates to the Cooper Park, destroyed in 1980 when the relief road was built,

have been replaced by the Elgin Fund and named the Harrison Gate after the three generations of the Harrison family who ran Johnstons of Elgin.

ONE OF THE MANY ROMAN DENARII FOUND AT BIRNIE 2005   ZZZ04334 (Mary Byatt)

FLOODS

The Lossie, Elgin's river, which for centuries provided energy for its mills and established its prosperity, continues to flood and cause trouble in the town. There have been two serious floods in the last few years. In November 2002, people who had just settled down again after being forced out of their homes by floods in 1997 found themselves once more living with friends or in rented accommodation.

Although Elgin was first built on a plateau above the river, it has expanded over the river's flood plain, much of which has been built on or covered in tarmac for car parking. Following the flood in 2002, a firm of engineers were asked to suggest possible schemes for flood relief, and they came up with three. One was the construction of high dams to hold back floodwater south of Elgin and release it slowly. Another was to carve a huge tunnel through the ridge to the north of Elgin and direct the floodwater to the reclaimed land that was once the Loch of Spynie. The third option, and the one that was accepted after public consultation, was to lengthen some of Elgin's lovely old stone bridges, raise the riverbanks though parts of Elgin, and demolish some of the industrial and other buildings on the flood plain. Future disruption is unavoidable, and the town will look very different.

Be that as it may, Elgin will still be a fine place to live, with a plentiful supply of shops and easy access to the surrounding countryside

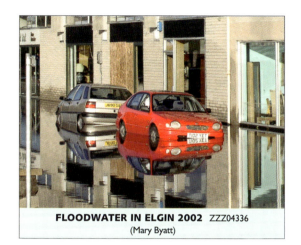

FLOODWATER IN ELGIN 2002 ZZZ04336
(Mary Byatt)

and to the sea. The short dark days of winter are more than compensated for by the long, sunny days of summer, when you can read the newspaper outside at midnight. This is, after all, Scotland's Riviera.

Elgin's Weekly Newspaper

Elgin's newspaper, The Northern Scot, has won a hat trick of awards since the millennium. It was named Highlands and Islands Local Newspaper of the Year in 2001, then the BT Scottish

Newspaper of the Year, and finally the BT UK Weekly Newspaper of the Year in 2002. Its editor was awarded the Barron Trophy in 2003; this trophy is awarded for excellence and outstanding journalism in the Highlands and Islands over a long period. The Barron Trophy was first donated in 1950 by Evan Barron, editor of the Inverness Courier. The photograph shows compositors and linotype operators at work in the former premises at 175 High Street.

OLD PRINTING PRESSES IN THE NORTHERN SCOT WORKS c1955 ZZZ04335
(Reproduced by kind permission of the Editor, The Northern Scot)

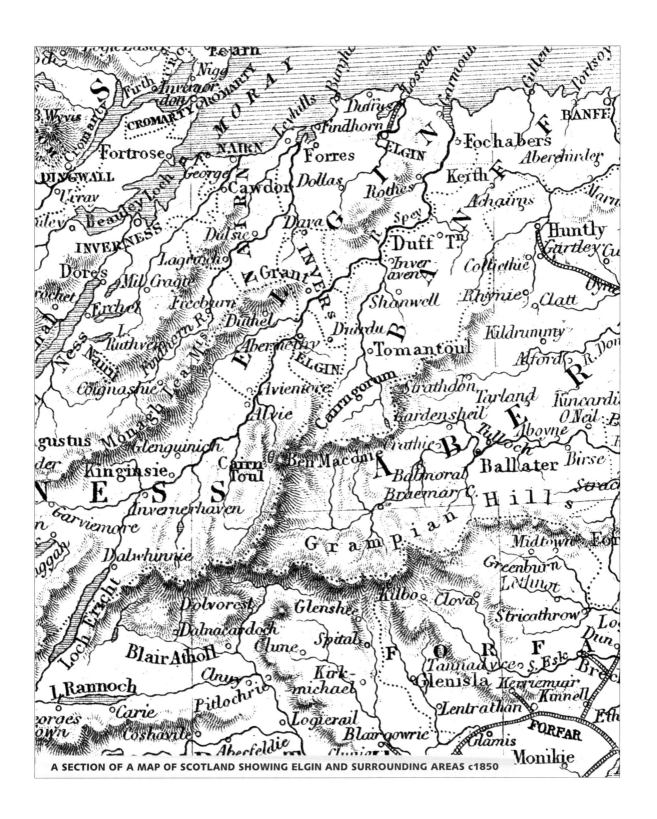

A SECTION OF A MAP OF SCOTLAND SHOWING ELGIN AND SURROUNDING AREAS c1850

ACKNOWLEDGEMENTS
Thanks to David Addison, Curator of the Elgin Museum, and to Pauline Taylor, Editor of The Northern Scot, for permission to use their photographs. Also to Alan Wills, Archivist of Gordonstoun School, and to Heather Urquhart, for loan of old books. Thanks also to Graham Wilson of the Elgin Library, and Ian Keillar, for help with research, and to my daughter, Sarah, and Richard Bennett, for help with the text..

BIBLIOGRAPHY
Barclay-Harvey, Sir Malcolm: A History of the Great North of Scotland Railway. 1949
Bartlam, Bill and Keillar, Ian: World War II in Moray. Librario Press 2003
Bartlam, W A: Buildings in Elgin Past and Present. Moray Field Club Bulletin 1999
Bartlam, W A: Elgin Bridges over the River Lossie. Moray Field Club Bulletin 1997
Beaton, E: The Design and Building of Elgin Museum. Moray Field Club Bulletin 1990
Bennett, Richard: Elgin Academy 1801-2001. Moravian Press 2001
Bishop, Bruce B: Witchcraft Trials in Elgin, Morayshire, 1560-1734. 2001
Bishop, Bruce B: The Lands and People of Moray. Parts 1-8. 2001
Bishop, Bruce B: The Closes of Elgin. 2002
Cant R G: Old Elgin. The Elgin Society 1946
Cant, R G: Historic Elgin and its Cathedral. 1974
Douglas, Robert: Sons of Moray. 1930
Johnson, Samuel: A Journey to the Western Islands of Scotland. 1773
Johnston's of Elgin: Scottish Estate Tweeds. 1995
Mackean, Charles: The District of Moray, An Illustrated Architectural Guide. The Rutland Press 1987
Mackintosh, H B: Elgin Past and Present. J D Yeadon, Elgin 1914
Mackintosh, Lachlan: Elgin Past and Present, A Guide and History. Black, Walker & Grassie, Elgin 1891
Main, Jenny: Scotland in Old Photographs – Elgin. Sutton Publishing Ltd 1996
Main, Jenny: Scotland in Old Photographs - Elgin People. Sutton Publishing Ltd 1998
Moray, Province and People. The Scottish Society for Northern Studies 1993
Seton, Mike: Moray Past and Present. Moray District Libraries 1978
Seton, Mike: The Whisky Distilleries of Moray. Moray District Libraries 1980
Shaw, Lachlan: The History of the Province of Moray, Vol III. University of Glasgow 1882
Watson, W E: Elgin Schools and Schoolmasters. The Moravian Press Ltd, Elgin
Weir, Robert: Elgin City's Highland League Triumphs and Tragedy 1895-2000. 2001
Young, Robert: The Annals of Elgin. 1879

Ottakar's Bookshops

Ottakar's bookshops, the first of which opened in Brighton in 1988, can now be found in over 130 towns and cities across the United Kingdom. Expansion was gradual throughout the 1990s, but the chain has expanded rapidly in recent years, with many new shop openings and the acquisition of shops from James Thin and Hammicks.

Ottakar's has always known that a shop's local profile is as important, if not more important, than the chain's national profile, and has encouraged its staff to make their shops a part of the local community, tailoring stock to suit the area and forging links with local schools and businesses.

Local history has always been a strong area for Ottakar's, and the company has published its own award winning local history titles, based on text written by its customers, in recent years.

With a reputation for friendly, intelligent and enthusiastic booksellers, warm, inviting shops with an excellent range of books and related products, Ottakar's is now one of the UK's most popular booksellers. In 2003 and then again in 2004 it won the prestigious Best Bookselling Company of the Year Award at the British Book Awards.

Ottakar's has commissioned The Francis Frith Collection to create a series of town history books similar to this volume, as well as a range of stylish gift products, all illustrated with historical photographs.

Participating Ottakar's bookshops can be found in the following towns and cities:

Aberdeen	Douglas, Isle of Man	Kendal	St Helier
Abergavenny	Dumfries	King's Lynn	Salisbury
Aberystwyth	Dundee	Kirkcaldy	Sheffield
Andover	East Grinstead	Lancaster	Stafford
Ashford	Eastbourne	Lincoln	Staines
Ayr	Elgin	Llandudno	Stevenage
Banbury	Enfield	Loughborough	Sutton Coldfield
Barnstaple	Epsom	Lowestoft	Teddington
Basildon	Falkirk	Luton	Tenterden
Berkhamsted	Fareham	Lymington	Tiverton
Bishop's Stortford	Farnham	Maidenhead	Torquay
Boston	Folkestone	Maidstone	Trowbridge
Brentwood	Glasgow	Market Harborough	Truro
Bromley	Gloucester	Milton Keynes	Tunbridge Wells
Bury St Edmunds	Greenwich	Newport	Twickenham
Camberley	Grimsby	Newton Abbot	Walsall
Canterbury	Guildford	Norwich	Wilmslow and
Carmarthen	Harrogate	Oban	Alderley Edge
Chatham	Hastings	Ormskirk	Wells
Chelmsford	Haywards Heath	Petersfield	Weston-super-Mare
Cheltenham	Hemel Hempstead	Portsmouth	Windsor
Cirencester	High Wycombe	Poole	Witney
Coventry	Horsham	Redhill	Woking
Crawley	Huddersfield	St Albans	Worcester
Darlington	Inverness	St Andrews	Yeovil
Dorchester	Isle of Wight	St Neots	

Francis Frith
Pioneer Victorian Photographer

Francis Frith, founder of the world-famous photographic archive, was a complex and multi-talented man. A devout Quaker and a highly successful Victorian businessman, he was philosophical by nature and pioneering in outlook. By 1855 he had already established a wholesale grocery business in Liverpool, and sold it for the astonishing sum of £200,000, which is the equivalent today of over £15,000,000. Now in his thirties, and captivated by the new science of photography, Frith set out on a series of pioneering journeys up the Nile and to the Near East.

He was the first photographer to venture beyond the sixth cataract of the Nile. Africa was still the mysterious 'Dark Continent', and Stanley and Livingstone's historic meeting was a decade into the future. The conditions for picture taking confound belief. He laboured for hours in his wicker dark-room in the sweltering heat of the desert, while the volatile chemicals fizzed dangerously in their trays. Back in London he exhibited his photographs and was 'rapturously cheered' by members of the Royal Society. His reputation as a photographer was made overnight.

By the 1870s the railways had threaded their way across the country, and Bank Holidays and half-day Saturdays had been made obligatory by Act of Parliament. All of a sudden the working man and his family were able to enjoy days out, take holidays, and see a little more of the world.

With typical business acumen, Francis Frith foresaw that these new tourists would enjoy having souvenirs to commemorate their days out. For the next thirty years he travelled the country by train and by pony and trap, producing fine photographs of seaside resorts and beauty spots that were keenly bought by millions of Victorians. These prints were painstakingly pasted into family albums and pored over during the dark nights of winter, rekindling precious memories of summer excursions. Frith's studio was soon supplying retail shops all over the country, and by 1890 F Frith & Co had become the greatest specialist photographic publishing company in the world, with over 2,000 sales outlets, and pioneered the picture postcard.

Francis Frith had died in 1898 at his villa in Cannes, his great project still growing. By 1970 the archive he created contained over a third of a million pictures showing 7,000 British towns and villages.

Frith's legacy to us today is of immense significance and value, for the magnificent archive of evocative photographs he created provides a unique record of change in the cities, towns and villages throughout Britain over a century and more. Frith and his fellow studio photographers revisited locations many times down the years to update their views, compiling for us an enthralling and colourful pageant of British life and character.

We are fortunate that Frith was dedicated to recording the minutiae of everyday life. For it is this sheer wealth of visual data, the painstaking chronicle of changes in dress, transport, street layouts, buildings, housing and landscape that captivates us so much today, offering us a powerful link with the past and with the lives of our ancestors.

Computers have now made it possible for Frith's many thousands of images to be accessed almost instantly. The archive offers every one of us an opportunity to examine the places where we and our families have lived and worked down the years. Its images, depicting our shared past, are now bringing pleasure and enlightenment to millions around the world a century and more after his death. For further information visit: www.francisfrith.co.uk

FREE PRINT OF YOUR CHOICE

Mounted Print
Overall size 14 x 11 inches (355 x 280mm)

Choose any Frith photograph in this book.
Simply complete the Voucher opposite and return it with your remittance for £2.25 (to cover postage and handling) and we will print the photograph of your choice in SEPIA (size 11 x 8 inches) and supply it in a cream mount with a burgundy rule line (overall size 14 x 11 inches).
Please note: photographs with a reference number starting with a "Z" are not Frith photographs and cannot be supplied under this offer.
Offer valid for delivery to one UK address only.

PLUS: Order additional Mounted Prints at HALF PRICE - £7.49 each (normally £14.99)
If you would like to order more Frith prints from this book, possibly as gifts for friends and family, you can buy them at half price (with no additional postage and handling costs).

PLUS: Have your Mounted Prints framed
For an extra £14.95 per print you can have your mounted print(s) framed in an elegant polished wood and gilt moulding, overall size 16 x 13 inches (no additional postage and handling required).

IMPORTANT!

These special prices are only available if you use this form to order . You must use the ORIGINAL VOUCHER on this page (no copies permitted). We can only despatch to one UK address. This offer cannot be combined with any other offer.

Send completed Voucher form to:
The Francis Frith Collection, Frith's Barn, Teffont, Salisbury, Wiltshire SP3 5QP

CHOOSE A PHOTOGRAPH FROM THIS BOOK

Voucher for FREE and Reduced Price Frith Prints

Please do not photocopy this voucher. Only the original is valid, so please fill it in, cut it out and return it to us with your order.

Picture ref no	Page no	Qty	Mounted @ £7.49	Framed + £14.95	Total Cost £
		1	Free of charge*	£	£
			£7.49	£	£
			£7.49	£	£
			£7.49	£	£
			£7.49	£	£
			£7.49	£	£

Please allow 28 days for delivery.
Offer available to one UK address only

* Post & handling	£2.25
Total Order Cost	£

Title of this book . . . .

I enclose a cheque/postal order for £ . . . .
made payable to 'The Francis Frith Collection'

OR please debit my Mastercard / Visa / Maestro / Amex card, details below

Card Number

Issue No (Maestro only)   Valid from (Maestro)

Expires   Signature

Name Mr/Mrs/Ms . . . .
Address . . . .
. . . .
. . . .
. . . . Postcode . . . .
Daytime Tel No . . . .
Email . . . .

ISBN: 1-84567-744-7   Valid to 31/12/08